An Early *Light*

In Gods Hands
Janice Gassi

An Early *Light*

Janice Tassi

Copyright © 2015 by Janice Tassi.

Library of Congress Control Number:	2015912631
ISBN: Hardcover	978-1-5035-9280-3
Softcover	978-1-5035-9279-7
eBook	978-1-5035-9278-0

All rights reserved. No part of this book may be reproduced or transmitted in any form or by any means, electronic or mechanical, including photocopying, recording, or by any information storage and retrieval system, without permission in writing from the copyright owner.

Any people depicted in stock imagery provided by Thinkstock are models, and such images are being used for illustrative purposes only.
Certain stock imagery © Thinkstock.

Print information available on the last page.

Rev. date: 08/07/2015

To order additional copies of this book, contact:
Xlibris
1-888-795-4274
www.Xlibris.com
Orders@Xlibris.com
716301

CONTENTS

Acknowledgements ix
Introduction xi
Chapter One: Actions of Others 1
Chapter Two: Our Last Good-Bye 5
Chapter Three: Jordan's River 8
Chapter Four: An Early Light 19
Chapter Five: The Gifts 27
Chapter Six: A Million Thoughts 41
Chapter Seven: The Painful Journey 48
Chapter Eight: Dragon Lady 52
Chapter Nine: Today You Became a Wife 64
Chapter Ten: Two Steps Forward 68
Chapter Eleven: Friendships 71
Chapter Twelve: Balloon Story 78
Chapter Thirteen: Tidbits 85
Chapter Fourteen: Poetry 92
Chapter Fifteen: Memories 100
Chapter Sixteen: Off the Richter Scale 112
Chapter Seventeen: Today 116
Chapter Eighteen: God's Timing 127

Epilogue 133
Epilogue II 136

I dedicate this book to you, Kelly Dawn. You gave me the stories. I may be the writer, but you are the author. I don't ask the big why anymore, Kelly. I know that it's because of who you are and how you have lived your life.

Acknowledgements

*T*hank you first to our Lord and Savior for all things and for keeping his promise to be there for us. All things are possible through him. He gets the glory!

To Kelly for inspiring me every day and for having a love that keeps on giving.

To my guardians, my messengers, you are awesome!

To family and friends who offered so much love and support during our darkest time. Each one of you in your own way helped us through the valley.

To Shannon Ewing and Laura Roberts for the beautiful programs, for the memorial service, and for the poster of Kelly's life for the reception.

To the collaborative efforts of the Storey County Fire Department, Brown Elementary, and Darin's and Kelly's community of friends, who put so much time, love, and expense into a beautiful service and reception for our daughter.

To Darin, Kelly loved you so much and had loved being your wife. She had looked forward to building a future and family together with you. Thank you for honoring Kelly through your choices and decisions pertaining to her and her family. Take all you say she taught you and you will find your peace. God bless you and your future.

To all of Kelly's friends and coworkers, thank you for your love and care. You all made up her days, and I know she had felt privileged to have had you in them.

To Washoe County, a big thank-you for all your hard work and dedication in seeking justice for our daughter.

Denielle, there are no words to express the gratitude we have for a stranger who sat on a lonely corner with our Kelly for almost three hours so she wouldn't be alone. Thank you for protecting her and letting her feel your presence. God had placed you there for Kelly and for us. All our love to you always.

Shannon, you have done an invaluable service for me putting this together in your computer. The time we spent together on this did not seem like work (to me, anyway); it was more like a bonding experience. We might have shared a few tears together, but there was a whole lot of laughter too. I'm glad you find me so entertaining, and I appreciate you not throwing me down the stairs, which I am sure you will do by the time we get through with this. I thank you for your trust, your confidence, and your expertise on the use of the computer. You amaze me with the talent you have in the operation of one of these things. Thank you for being a dear best friend to Kelly and for the love you have given to all of us. I couldn't love you more.

Introduction

I have always been a very private person, sharing the personal parts of my life with only a select few, and I'd felt the walls in our home will protect our privacy from the outside world. The night of August 13, 2003, those walls could not shield our lives from the public. They learned of one of the most intimate and personal parts of our lives: the death of our daughter Kelly Dawn. There were so many calls to be made, and I remember screaming to my husband, Randy, "Don't tell them that Kelly died!" I thought I could keep this a secret. I wanted to protect Kelly's privacy and ours. Well, I couldn't, and it wasn't going to be. It was on the Reno news and in the Reno newspaper (Kelly lived in Reno, and we live in Susanville, eighty-six miles north of Reno) and our local radio station and newspaper. Everybody knew—we were going to have to move. Everywhere we'd go, people would know something so personal of us. It would be months before I went out to our local stores and businesses. I remember, the first time someone approached me, I put a hand up and cried, "Please, I need to shop. I can't talk." The sweet lady I had known for years simply said, "Can I give you a hug?"

I found myself going to places where I knew there wouldn't be great volumes of people, like in small gift shops to do some holiday gift shopping. Susanville is a small community where everyone knows practically everyone. I was a grocery clerk for many years at a local supermarket, so I knew just about everyone, and they knew me. As it turned out, I grew to be grateful to the people of this community who offered so much love and support. My life, I felt, was an open book, and I started sharing the personal experiences that had come before and after the loss of our Kelly. The ones that gave us comfort and hope. More and more, I started sharing these stories. The walls were coming down, and I wanted to welcome others on a journey to hope and peace. Presentation was important to Kelly, so I want to present this in a way that would have pleased her.

Chapter One

Actions of Others

Kelly Dawn was born to us on November 18, 1978. She was born on the same day as the Jonestown murders or suicide. She was truly a blessing to her family, friends, and community. She was the youngest of three children. Ted was her older brother by six years, and Angel her sister by five years. She entered this world six weeks premature. I had the threat of a miscarriage with her, but by taking a pregnancy leave and using all the precautions, I was able to take her to almost full term. She was delivered by C-section at Lassen Memorial by our family physician. He had used caution by calling ahead to Washoe Medical Center in Reno, Nevada, for Care Flight. Lassen Memorial was not equipped for urgent care of pediatric patients. Kelly was care-flighted to Washoe Medical Center with various complications. She overcame her struggles and was able to go home nine days later. Kelly was taken from us on Wednesday, August 13, 2003. She left us unable to put up the same fight in death as she had in birth. It was instant; she didn't see it coming.

Kelly Berry and her husband of nearly four months, Darin Berry, were walking home from a neighborhood 7-Eleven convenience store. It was a beautiful summer evening. Kelly had just had her wisdom teeth pulled out the previous Friday and felt a cold Slurpee would soothe her gums. Kelly and Darin usually took the shortcut to 7-Eleven by crossing the field behind their house, but Kelly felt like going the long way for the walk. She and Darin had just bought a new home in the foothills south of Reno. Kelly grew up surrounded by mountains and chose to have the Virginia foothills out her back door and Mount Rose as her view from the front. They lived on Gold Run Road, off Toll Road, a main entrance to the subdivision where they lived. Toll Road to Gold Run was a pretty lengthy walk, but it was a straight road with a dirt bank to walk on. Kelly and Darin were on the right side of the road, but Darin said traffic was pretty heavy and people were traveling too fast. He and Kelly sensed danger, so they moved to the left side of the road and walked in the bank, facing traffic. They were off the road on a fairly wide dirt shoulder when a Ryder truck approached them at high speed and was too close for comfort. Darin moved Kelly to his left to protect her.

According to Darin, they had stopped to enjoy the view of Mount Rose and the gorgeous sunset. Darin and Kelly shared a kiss and hugged before they continued their walk home. Darin recalled that Kelly said that he would always be loved and taken care of if something would happen to her. He brushed off what she said and replied that they needed to get home and told her not to talk that way. Did Kelly sense something was about to happen? What happened next happened so quickly and began the nightmare that would change so many lives forever. Darin said he heard gravel crunching, and before he and Kelly could turn around, they were struck from behind by a small-sized Toyota truck driven by a thirty-nine-year-old man high on drugs. Darin was thrown to the side, but Kelly was carried on the hood of the truck, for over 150 feet, which then hit the curb, and Kelly flew off, landing on the pavement of Gold Run Road. She suffered from a broken neck as well as other injuries and landed on her temple. Kelly was killed instantly. She was gone from us.

The man who did this to our beautiful daughter passed out, crossed over diagonally to the other side of the road, and hit them. It was like hell on earth! He took our baby from us. Kelly's brother, Ted, and sister, Angel, like us, were forced to live this life of pain and suffering. Darin lost a future with the love he chose to share it with. Darin suffered leg fractures that have now healed. The healing over the loss of his new wife was slow in coming, but time was our healer, God our comforter.

Before Clyde struck Kelly and Darin, he was approached by a car in the opposite lane. The lady in the car swerved to avoid a head-on collision. She witnessed the accident in her rearview mirror. A young boy on his bicycle also witnessed the horrible scene and was almost hit. I pray that they have found comfort. I am sure this lady would have done anything to prevent what had happened to Kelly and Darin from happening here. She did what anyone of us would have done—swerved. That was a night of horrifying magnitude for both. I have thought of them often and hope that they have found their peace.

Darin lost his father to cancer when he was seven years old. He loved his father-in-law and said he was happy to have a father again after all these years. That night at the hospital, we went to see Darin. The first thing I said to him was "You are not going to lose another daddy."

Clyde, this faceless stranger, had been in a single-car accident earlier the same day. He rolled his car three times after what he said was a sneezing fit. Hmm. He was taken to Washoe Medical Center, checked out, and released with no obvious injuries. Unlike alcohol, drugs can go undetected. Unless you are suspected of it, you cannot be tested for it. That is one of those protected rights. The law does not require officers to prove the driver is under the influence of drugs. He was picked up by a friend and transported to his father's house. Ninety minutes later, he borrowed his father's truck to return to his home on Toll Road.

When questioned by his lawyer while on the stand for the pretrial, he was asked, "Why did you get back in a vehicle so soon after the previous accident?"

He replied, "I wanted to get back in the saddle again."

He wanted to overcome his fear of driving! He wanted to go home to check on his dog. He said his last thought before hitting Kelly and Darin was that if he had his dog with him (in the earlier accident), his dog might have been killed, and that upset him. That was the last thing he remembered. According to the newspaper, Clyde McPotts (fictional name) was quoted as saying, "I blacked out, and when I came to I veered over and hit them. I must have killed her instantly. I got out, and there she was." Clyde was also quoted as saying that on his thirty-ninth birthday, he "partied like a rock star."

An affidavit, filed in support of an arrest warrant, alleged a blood draw taken after the accident revealed Clyde had five times the statutory limit of marijuana in his blood and nearly twice the limit of methamphetamine. Investigators allegedly found 0.08 grams of methamphetamine in a backpack in the truck. Witnesses and investigators from the first crash said, "Clyde showed no signs of drug or alcohol-related impairment, authorities said."

I want to share with you that Darin, aged twenty-four, was a Storey County firefighter. He returned to work after months of rehabilitation but now works for Sparks Fire Department. It's been over two years now, and he has since sold his and Kelly's home and bought a new home in Sparks, Nevada. He is getting on with his life and is in a new relationship. We support him, but yes, it is hard. We don't want to lose Darin, but we know he must move on. I believe he will always be a part of our lives in some way, but we know it won't be as constant. This is painful! He was Kelly's husband—he always will be to us!

From the time Kelly was a little girl, she had dreamed of going to college. Getting an education was very important to her. School wasn't always easy for her, but she was very disciplined and very determined. She did go to college and got her bachelor's degree in criminal justice. She graduated from the University of Nevada, Reno, in December 2002. She got a job at the courthouse as a court service officer. Part of her job was helping those with alcohol and drug addiction. She lost her life at the hands of the very person she was trying to help. At her memorial, a gentleman came to pay his respects. He said Kelly helped him overcome his addiction. If you can just save one, that's what matters. She did.

Chapter Two

Our Last Good-Bye

Over the Fourth of July weekend, Kelly wanted to visit Angel and her family in Meridian, Idaho, but the plane ticket costs more money than Kelly had anticipated, so she didn't think she would be able to go. Angel said, "If we pay the extra money, will you come?" Kelly took the flight. The two sisters shared a special weekend together. Kelly had shared her concerns with Angel that she felt she wouldn't be able to have children. Angel said, "I will carry Aubrey Faith for you if you can't." This shows the love between the two sisters. Then, they always said their good-byes with "I love you," "No, I love you more." They couldn't have loved each other more. Angel says, "There are no good-byes, just a great big hello when we see her again."

July 11 was my and Randy's anniversary. It was his day off, and we wanted to go to Reno for dinner. I told Kelly of our plans, but knowing it was Darin's day off and they had so little time together, we didn't want them to change any plans for us. With Darin being a firefighter and it being the height of fire season, they didn't see a whole lot of each other. Kelly agreed. That Friday (July 11) morning, Kelly called and asked me to let them join us for dinner; it was what she and Darin wanted. They never missed an opportunity to spend time with us. I told her as long as they wouldn't try to pay for dinner, we would love for them to join us. They were both so generous of their time, their love, and their little means. We met at a local restaurant and shared dinner and a wonderful time together. Randy picked up the tab, but Kelly and Darin had prearranged the payment for the dinner. That was the last time Randy spent time with his little girl. Thank you, Kelly and Darin. It was the best! We now celebrate that memory.

As I've mentioned earlier, Kelly had her wisdom teeth pulled Friday before the accident. I spent the weekend with her to take care of her. I went to Reno Thursday night after picking Ted up from the airport (he also lives in Boise). He had to attend a wedding in Susanville. Ted and I shared dinner and a wonderful evening of conversation with Kelly. Kelly and I went to her dental appointment the next morning, and Ted headed to Susanville. I got to be a mommy to her, fixing her soup, watching movies with her, and cleaning her beautiful home while she slept. Kelly and Darin had just gotten a puppy that same day. Kelly wanted to break in a puppy first before she had children. She wanted a dog as a family pet. Darin named him Gunner. Occasionally, when our kids would have injuries, I would get them a boo-boo gift. For having her wisdom teeth pulled, I bought Kelly a small statue of a little girl jumping over the back of a little boy (like leapfrog). I told Kelly, "That's Aubrey Faith and Mason Graham," the names she had already picked out for her future children.

On Sunday, Ted's flight was to leave Reno at 8:00 p.m. Instead of having a friend drop him off at the airport, he chose to be dropped off at Kelly's and spent an extra hour with his sister before he left. I dropped him off at the airport on my way home to Susanville. As Ted and I got ready to leave, I headed to the truck and left Ted and Kelly alone. As I waited, I had this urge to go back in the house and give Kelly one more hug and say good-bye, but I refrained and let them have some time together. That was our last time together. I called Kelly on the cell phone as I headed out of Reno. I called to say "I miss you already." It was like I knew I was going to miss her for the rest of my life.

When I got home, I called to let Kelly know I had made it safely. We had been talking for quite a while when she got another call. It was her brother calling from the airport to tell her that she made him want to make some changes in his life. Ted struggled with alcohol but wanted her to know that he would not have another drink until they got together for Thanksgiving. They would then share a glass of wine.

I want to share all this with you. We all had our last special time together. We got to share our love for one another, Kelly and us. We got to say our last good-bye. Thank you, God. No regrets, no missed opportunities.

Chapter Three

Jordan's River

There have been so many things that have been brought to light since Kelly's passing. I want to share these experiences in the hope that you or anyone else will find comfort in these stories. After the loss of our Kelly, we were so desperate to find comfort any way we could. I bought as many inspirational books as I could get my hands on. I've always believed in God and heaven, but faith was not enough for me. I needed to know that her life did not end, not now, not so young, not before it got started. If I read a whole book and only got one thing out of it, it was worth reading.

There is one book I remember reading, but don't ask me the name of it; I can't remember. I was in such a state of shock and lived under this umbrella of fog that I had little recall of so much information. What I do remember though is a statement made by a grieving mother who had lost her daughter tragically at a young age also. She said it's like she (the mother) had left this world and would pay a visit occasionally but was gone again into the world of grieving. As time went on, she stayed a little longer here, until one day she did not leave. She was back among the living. That explained how I felt. I was here physically, but emotionally, I was gone. My thoughts were of Kelly 24-7—Kelly, Kelly, Kelly, an all-consuming pain and loss. You can't escape it; you have to live through it.

Grieving is the same for all of us, yet how we grieve is different. It's the one thing in this life that we can't ask of another—"Grieve for me." I would've shared with you the order of the grieving process, except there isn't one. A few people have informed me of the grieving process: shock, denial, hate, anger, hopelessness, anxiety, and sadness. It's different and in a different order for everyone. I was all over the place. My grieving process was a mangled mess. "How come I am feeling this, and when is that going to kick in?" It's like a waiting game. "When will it start, and when will it end? What do you do with hate?" I had to set it aside. I didn't know what to do with it. Anger, now that one was no problem. I was not only angry for the obvious reasons, but I was also angry with anyone who had ever hurt Kelly. I became consumed with anger. Kelly's hurts generally came from those she trusted. She was always so forgiving. After we lost her, I wasn't.

I didn't feel I could turn to God. He had taken her from us. I wanted to know what we had done that was so bad that he would take Kelly from us. I know, looking back, I was dumb in my thinking, but it was one of the first questions I had asked of God on that August night. I had prayed so hard for the health and safety of our children. I wanted the why answered. I know it won't be in this life. I just have to believe he had a darn good reason. Faith is not always easy. It forces us to believe in what we can't see or understand.

I spent so much time being angry with God. I deliberately used his name in vain, something I never intentionally did, and if I did, I suffered so with the guilt of it. I wanted to hurt God like he had hurt us. I was so blinded by anger I almost missed his gifts. God says that when we suffer, he is the first one there for us. I believe he was there even before the night of August 13. I believe he was with me that very morning.

I was in the bathroom, getting ready for the day. I was taking my nephew Jesse to the matinee movie *Freaky Friday*. While I was getting ready, I started humming the song "Michael, Row the Boat Ashore." I thought to myself, *Now, why in the world am I humming this song?* I hadn't heard or thought of that song in many years. A short time later, I turned on the TV in our bedroom to keep me company while I finished getting ready. I don't know what channel I had on or what program I was listening to. I just wanted company. After a few minutes, I heard the song "Michael, Row the Boat Ashore" on TV. Not the whole song, just that verse. I thought to myself, *Whoa, I was just humming that song. What are the odds of that?*

At one o'clock in the morning, after learning the news of our daughter Kelly's death, Randy and I headed to Reno with my brother Larry and sister-in-law Debbie. We were going to see Darin. We could help Darin. Halfway to Reno, in the Doyle area, I looked out the truck's side window, wrenched in pain and still hearing the noises coming out of me. I had never heard those sounds before. I didn't know at first they were coming from me. I didn't know the body could make such a sound. It was my soul crying. I had never cried from my soul before. Those cries haunted me even months later. Not yet knowing the details of the accident, I started visualizing all kinds of awful things. I visualized Kelly crawling and crying out for me; and then there it was, the song "Michael, Row the Boat Ashore." I was humming the song again. I turned desperately to Randy, Larry, and Debbie. "Do you know this song? Do you know what it means?" I then shared with them the experience that I had that morning with the song. My mind-set then was this: how could I have been humming a song? I became afraid of the song. I thought it represented something bad. I had learned the lyrics years ago but, in my despair, had forgotten them. It would be weeks later before I would investigate the song and what it meant. I couldn't let it go. The song goes like this (because of copyright issues, I have to shorten this version):

Michael, Row the Boat Ashore

The river is deep and the river is wide, hallelujah
Milk and honey on the other side, hallelujah
Jordan's river is chilly and cold, hallelujah
Chills the body but not the soul, hallelujah

Now I will take you back a few years, when Kelly was attending UNR. She was going through a difficult time in her life, partly attributed to a few tough years here at home before she moved to Reno. She was seeing a counselor at UNR who was helping her through her difficulties.

On March 15, 1993, Randy came home from work and told us that the mill he had worked in for ten years was closing down. He was going to be out of job. We really needed the income that my job (grocery clerk/checker) provided. The following year, everything shut down for me physically. After nineteen years and what my doctor determined was accumulative trauma, I was unable to perform my job anymore. This time, it involved lawyers, state doctors, workers' compensation, and let's just say the actions of another kept me from getting the medical and financial help I needed.

After two years, I quit the fight and my job. I had to consider my health and what the stress of all this was doing to all of us. It was a very involved case that I won't share in the same pages of this book. I can only tell you that I was affected emotionally as well as physically, and Randy and Kelly witnessed an all-consumed, angry, depressed me. Randy, the pessimist, has always felt we are all just a number, but I will argue that no, we aren't; we all do matter. I hated that he was right. What bothered me most was learning later on how Kelly was affected by it all. Today I have gotten the help I needed so long ago—the MRIs and x-rays I was denied in 1994 and a diskography. It revealed the problems causing the pain, including two disks that were bone to bone, and it showed I had no cushion left in either one. I am looking forward to the surgery that will relieve the pain I have been suffering with. By the way, my neurologist's name is Michael Song.

Randy, after months of applying and being denied one job after another (not easy at age forty-eight to find employment), pursued a job at High Desert State Prison. He was hired in 1996, and it was a blessing. It took us years to pay off the debts from these three long years. We just had to sit, wait, and trust God. He knew exactly what he was doing with us.

It was Kelly's senior year, and we had no money for yearbooks, prom dresses, or special activities, such as the senior trip. Kelly never complained, but it hurt her dad and me that after all those years of hard work, we were in financial devastation and couldn't provide these things for her. Randy did anything and everything to pay the mortgage. Shortly after my injury on August 18, after being denied workers' compensation, I did sign up for state compensation, but the money paid to me soon ran out. By the love and grace of some family members, Kelly did get that prom dress, and her senior trip was paid for. She so deserved it and more.

Studies came first for Kelly, even before boys. She graduated with honors, was in the top 10 percent of her class, and was so proud of her honor cords on graduation day. Pretty impressive for someone who started out at the special help table in her early years. Kelly got herself a job at Honey Lake Photography. She paid for her classes and books at Lassen Community College. We couldn't help her financially, and she applied for but did not receive any scholarships. She would call from work on payday and ask, "Do we need any groceries?" Do you know how much pride we had to swallow to accept this assistance from our daughter? We accepted her offer. Later on, when I apologized to Kelly for having her go through such a tough time with us and seeing how affected she was by it all, she replied, "It was an honor, Mom." What a great gift of words she gave me. When I look back on it all to this day, I hear her say "It was an honor." I love her so, and I miss her every minute of every day. This is all so painful, even the beautiful parts. But the tears won't stop me; I have to get this done.

As I was saying, Kelly was seeing a counselor at University of Nevada, Reno. This time I spoke of came back to haunt her, and the counselor told her, "It's like you, your mom, and your dad were out to sea, and you had to make it back to shore on a dinghy." I had learned all this from Kelly the night before I was to catch a flight to Denver, Colorado, for the birth of our first grandchild in 1999. I didn't want to leave Kelly. When I got to Angel's, I shared with her what was going on with Kelly and told her I needed to find something for her. She asked what, and I said, "I don't know. I will know it when I see it." I was looking for a boo-boo gift, I guess. In the second shop I went into, I found it. It was a Boyds Bear snow globe. It had Mama and Papa Bear, in their sailor suits, inside the globe, a periscope in Mama's hand and a ship in Papa's. Baby Bear was on top of the snow globe, reclining, with his hand on a miniature globe. It sat on an old trunk (a replica of those from years ago), with a tag that read as follows:

> From the ends of the earth and back
> USS *Friendship*
> Contents friendship handle with care
> Best friends always ship together
> Around the world and through thick and thin

It was musical and played the tune "Anchors Aweigh." I found what I was looking for. I mailed it with a letter to Kelly and shared the significance of the globe and what it meant to me. That was Mom and Dad on the inside, and she was guiding us to shore.

I believe that was the significance of the song "Michael, Row the Boat Ashore." God was letting us know Kelly had made it to shore, to the land of milk and honey. There was also a letter that Kelly had written to her dad and me before her wedding day. We received it in the mail upon the return trip from her wedding. Before she started her married life, she wanted to thank us for her childhood.

Dear Mom and Dad,

I will never be able to express how lucky I am to have been blessed with the both of you. With every day of my life, I have always felt your love, support, and encouragement. Whether I was filled with excitement to show you my report card or tell you that I passed my hunter safety class or had to confess that there was damage done for the second time to your new truck (while in my possession), you were there for me. You have been my backboard and have held me up when I did not have the strength.

What I want the two of you to know is that I love my life! You gave me a childhood filled with precious memories and are responsible for the person I have become. As Darin and I begin our new journey as husband and wife, we will have your marriage as an inspiration and as a model to guide us through the difficult times as well as to remind us that each moment shared is irreplaceable.

As I look at our ship, it is stronger than ever and is pleasantly sailing through life. Only the future can reveal what the sea has in store for us. What I do know is that come rough or calm waters, our family will always conquer all because the two of you have taught us to fight for love and to fight for each other.

Thank you for having enriched my life in every way!

*Love,
Your little girl, Kelly*

I had questioned God many times during that dark time in 1994: "Why, God? What is this all about? What is your plan for us?" I came to believe it was to strengthen us for an even darker time. He gave me the wisdom to leave my job so I could spend more time with my family. I was given nine years of something with Kelly that I wouldn't have had otherwise. My job would never have allowed it. God knew he would be bringing her home sooner than we all expected, so he gave us the gift of time.

One night, around midnight, in the midst of all this joblessness, I looked out my kitchen window. We have a beautiful big pond/reservoir at the end of our property. The moon was just above the horizon of a small mountain range in the distance. The moon's reflection on the pond made a perfect line straight toward me. The perfect line soon turned into a perfect cross. I ran out on the deck to take a closer look at it. How did that happen? The only thing that I could figure out was that some ducks had crossed that line in just the right spot, and the moon had illuminated the wake they left behind to form a perfect cross. I had a cross on my pond! I trusted that God was letting me know he was there for us, and that put me on the road to recovery.

The morning following my cross on the pond, I called one of my dear friends, Nancy, to tell her what I had witnessed. Nancy had recently been diagnosed with cancer, and I wanted to share the hope. After a long courageous battle, she died in the spring of 2001. I wrote this poem for Nancy's birthday before she learned of her grim prognosis.

A Birthday Wish

Your birthday is a special day
Another year older—a gift, I'd say
You've traveled down many roads
At times carrying a heavy load
I'm proud of you in lots of ways
The way you fill your busy days
You give so much of yourself to others
To family, friends, and unfortunate brothers
I remember our children being young
We shared our lives, had some fun
I wouldn't change the years we spent
Being friends and what it meant
So peace is what I pray for you
A beautiful day, a smile or two
God bless you on your special day
My friend, as always, I want to say

That would be her last birthday. God bless you, my friend. Nancy had a great love for the Lord and had served him well. She had lost her husband, Mike, the year before to the same disease. Mike was a godly man. He and Nancy started Crossroads Ministries here in Susanville, and he would serve a sermon with a free meal. Most of the food was donated by Nancy and Mike themselves.

We (people) have an amazing survival mode in us. We had to survive for Ted and Angel. They needed us. They wouldn't make it without us. We had to help them. That is what Randy and I have been focusing on. We had done all the bargaining with God: "Why didn't you take one of us? We would have gladly traded places with Kelly. Aren't we supposed to go first?" She was so cheated. She wanted to be a wife and a mommy. She had worked so hard and had accomplished so much in her young life. It was all supposed to start paying off for her. But maybe God saw her accomplishments differently than us. Maybe she had fulfilled her purpose.

Kelly had one of the finest qualities of all, that being she was a very selfless person. She was so giving of herself to her family, friends, and acquaintances. She found her greatest pleasure was in doing for others. She very seldom took; she loved the gift of giving. In her sophomore year, one of her teachers—I think in English—asked each student to share a picture of themselves at a young age and then tell how they have changed since that time and age. This was her life, and these are her words from her essay:

> *Kelly Tassi, as seen in this picture at the age of seven, is celebrating the end of her second-grade year with a fun-filled day of many activities. The ribbon reflects an accomplishment of coming in second in a relay race. Life is a lot like that, a relay race. It's full of endurance, speed, pacing, momentum, balance, and well, staying on track! The rewards can be great if you follow the rules of the game of life.*
>
> *It never really took much to make me happy. I was and still am easy to please. I don't need to be entertained!*
>
> *My likes have been simple. I like spending time with my family. I like music and a good movie. I enjoy the outdoors, hunting, fishing, or going for a hike. I like spending time with my friends, just hanging out with them.*
>
> *I dislike reading (always have), bad news, negative people, and carrots.*
>
> *My fears have always been black, hollow, and cold. I have this fear of being alone. The age I was in the picture was a time*

of struggle for me in school. I had to work extra hard to keep from falling behind my class. I needed the help of a teacher's aide and had to sit at the extra help table. It was the fourth grade before I caught up with my classmates. Because of that struggle, I don't want to feel the pressures of falling behind in what I set out to do.

Kelly (in the picture) was never a leader, but I've never been a follower either. I was always a little shy, but I feel I have just about overcome that. I was a little timid and insecure; confidence was something I had to build over time. With the reassurance and coaching of my family, I grew to gain confidence in myself. I'm not over confident, but comfortable with myself. I've never liked being the center of attention. I am more comfortable outside the circle, just observing. I feel that I am learning more by looking from the outside in instead of the inside out.

I believe in living by the golden rule, as taught to me in my early years. I try to be respectful toward others and treat them the way I would like to be treated. I have high moral standards, and I try to live by them.

I have hopes and dreams. The hope of being surrounded by the love of my family. The hope of never losing the things that matter most in life to me. I give thanks to the Lord for the blessings I have been given each day of my life.

My dreams are always within reach if I work hard toward them. My dream is doing what brings others and me happiness. Dreams can be the simple pleasures of life. They come from being prepared for the challenges of life. I dream that I can fulfill the dreams of today and dream for tomorrow. Every day is a dream!

As I am approaching sweet sixteen, I can honestly say that I am very content and very happy with my life. This past year, I have met so many neat people who have become close friends. I'm doing a lot more socializing than I have done before. I continue to stay focused on school and my studies, but I make time for fun! I am looking forward to taking driver's training and getting my license!

JANICE TASSI

I have an older brother (Ted) and sister (Angel) who are both in the navy. Ted is stationed in Yorktown, Virginia, and Angel is stationed in Japan. They both joined the navy this last year. I really miss them, but we keep the communication lines open. I enjoy all the experiences that they share with me. I love all the navy paraphernalia I receive from them. A lot of people ask me if I plan to join the navy after high school. I believe that the navy has a lot to offer—education, life's learning experiences, seeing the world around us, and doing the duty of serving our country. However, the boot camp thing scares the daylights out of me, and I suffer from motion sickness.

Do I still have the child in me? Yes! I have the structure of my childhood. I have the happiness in my life and the joy in my heart. I have just tried to expand all that I was into who I am and who I will become. The journey of life has not taken me far from the child in the picture.

Chapter Four

An Early Light

On the night of the accident—I hate calling it that; this was no accident but a choice, a selfish, destructive choice that took our daughter's life—I received a phone call around 9:20 p.m. from a friend named Mike who works with Randy. He was very concerned about something he had heard at work.

"Is everything okay there?" he asked.

I said, "Yeah, everything is fine."

He said Randy's name was crossed off the schedule. They heard that something awful had happened.

I said, "No. Has Randy made it to work yet? He should be there by now."

Mike said no, but he would have Randy call me when he'd get to work.

The alarm had already gone off in me. Something about that phone call was unnerving. Our nephew Dan, who lives in Carson City, was spending the night with us, as he did every third Wednesday because of his job. I went to Dan and told him to talk to me and calm me down as something was not right. That's when I heard the key in the door (it sounded so loud). Randy was home. I knew it before he walked in that this was not good. He was crying like I'd never seen him cry before. My first thought was that it was his mother, but she lived right next door to us. How could he have found out before me?

He said Kelly and Darin were in a car accident, and Darin was at Washoe Medical Center with serious leg injuries.

I said, "Okay, let's go."

He said, "Kelly was killed."

I screamed, ran out the back door onto the deck, and tried to get on the railing. Dan pulled me back. I had to go to her. I didn't want her to be alone. I screamed "Kelly!" into the heavens. I couldn't breathe. I knelt in front of Randy. I couldn't help him. He couldn't help me.

Randy called my brother and said, "Get over here now. We need help."

It would be an hour before we could call Ted and Angel's spouses about the news. They were both at work. They were both RNs, as well as Ted. Ted and Angel were at their homes. A plan had to be constructed. Brian would need reinforcement when he'd approach Ted with this. Ted was very protective of his little sister. He would not be controlled. Brian and Ted's wife went together to deliver the news to Ted and Angel. We are so proud of how Brian and Ted's wife handled this.

At the hospital in the early morning hours, after we saw Darin, I asked a nurse there, "Where is Kelly?"

The nurse replied, "She's at the morgue. You go right through those doors."

My feet were cemented to the floor. I wanted so bad to go and be with her, but I couldn't go to my baby, not like this. I was in such a state of shock and denial. This wasn't happening! I knew I would not leave without Kelly, and she would not leave without me. From past experiences, I had viewed many friends after their passing and those in their final hours, and that was the last vision I had of them. The last time I saw Kelly, she was dressed in a lavender top, with her cute shorts and her hair clipped up. That was how I saw her. That was how I wanted to remember her.

Days later, at the mortuary, I had on those same concrete shoes.

The gentleman said, "I can take you to Kelly. She is upstairs. Take your time."

How about sixty years? I couldn't move, and neither could Randy. They had to do an autopsy on Kelly. None of us could go and see her like that—a decision we do not regret and know that Kelly would not have wanted for us. This choice may be difficult for some to understand, but it was our choice, and we have to live with that choice. We were to go through these double doors to pick out her box. She wanted to be cremated; we all had made that choice for ourselves years ago. We all wanted to know the other's wishes. I had to go through those doors. It was like stepping from one dimension into another. As I entered the room, the thought came to me (it wasn't my thought though; it was like it was given to me) that death is as natural as being born. Somehow, that gave me the strength to get the job done.

We got home at six thirty in the morning. Dan said he saw the accident on the news. We never watched any news. We didn't want to, and family members protected us from it. The first person to show up that morning was a neighbor by the name of Valerie. She walked in, took me by the hand, and with so much authority, led me out to the family room. I don't know what she said, if anything. She just let me talk and cry. I told her I was so angry and just wanted to hit something, and I didn't have a Ouiser (straight from the mouth of Sally Field in *Steel Magnolias*). I later shared this with some family members when Ted and my nephew Dan offered to go next door to get my mother-in-law, Dorothy. I will never forget Valerie's approach.

The phone never stopped ringing. The people kept coming, even some we had never met before. All the cards and food, so many gifts and donations, all this meant so much to us. It will never be forgotten. Family members who came and spent days with us, who did what we couldn't do. After learning about their sister, Ted, his wife, Angel, Brian, and the family drove all night (separate cars) and got there at around one o'clock the next afternoon. I have often thought of how that had to have been a trip from hell for them. We all had our own pains that night. When Ted and Angel walked through the front door, Angel said, "Please tell us it isn't true." Mom, dad, brother, and sister fell to a heap in the middle of the floor. Our chain had been broken—Kelly was missing. We will all, on our day, be linked back with Kelly. One by one, the chain will be reconnected. I have a plaque in a back bedroom that reads as follows:

Our family
Is a circle of strength and love
With every birth and every union the circle grows
Every joy shared adds more love
Every crisis faced together makes the circle stronger
[I can't make out the signature of the author]

My earliest memory of God's teachings came from my Grandma Jo, whom we would visit in Kansas. She would make us grandkids (seven of us) a glass of warm milk at night and would read us scriptures from the Bible. I enjoyed the words from the Good Book, but not the warm milk.

I remember a conversation I had with God (months after the loss of Kelly) when I had pleaded with him to spare us any more painful lessons. We didn't want to stop learning and growing; we just wanted the easy lessons, the painless ones.

The first night after Angel and Ted came home, at about four o'clock in the morning, Angel came into our bedroom (I'm sure, to check on Randy and me). We sat on the edge of the bed, and Angel told me that she wanted to have Kelly's Nomination bracelet. The next day, Angel and Ted went to Reno to see Darin. When Darin saw them, he sat up in bed and told Angel that Kelly had come to him in a dream and said to give Angel her Nomination bracelet. Darin was desperate for someone to go to his house and get that bracelet for Angel, and someone did. Angel came home that night shaking and pale. I thought we were going to have to take her to the hospital. Angel said, "Kelly heard me tell you about the bracelet."

We barely went to bed before 5:00 a.m. We were all surviving on very little sleep. How can you survive so many days on so little sleep? It must be the shock. Anyway, in the wee hours of the morning, I shared with Angel a secret I had kept from all of them since 1986. I went into what was once Angel and Kelly's bedroom and retrieved a framed photograph. The following is the story I shared with all of them that morning.

Back in 1986, after going through some recent pictures we had taken, I came across one of Kelly and me on a family outing to Mount Lassen. I was looking at the picture of the two of us when I felt compelled to write a heartfelt message on the back. I had never done this before on any other picture. The sentiment I had is the following:

AN EARLY LIGHT

Kelly,

I'll treasure this picture always as I will this moment
We sat almost on top of Mount Lassen.
Remember always how much I love you.
You warm my heart and fill it with laughter
And joy with your thoughtful, loving ways.
I thank God for you because you are a special gift,
Our gift from God.

I love you,
Mom

    After writing this, a voice in my head gently said, "But you will only have her for a little while." This frightened me, and I almost went to my knees. I answered with "What, is she going to get cancer or something?" I quickly put the picture in the frame I had bought for it. I never took that picture out of that frame again, nor did I tell anybody, including Kelly, what I had written or about what I had experienced that day of the writing. I was afraid I would hear that voice again. I shared this only after Kelly's passing. We did only have her for a little while.

In the early hours of the morning, while outside on the deck, we experienced a plague of dragonflies like you have never seen before. There were thunder and lightning storms and power outages. I spent one day chasing butterflies. They were everywhere. Our neighbor Dana came over later that day, and when I opened the door, she had on a beautiful butterfly necklace. I almost fell to the floor. I told her I had been chasing butterflies all day. She took that necklace off and put it on me. She wanted me to wear it. I told her I would return it in a few days. It wound up being a beautiful gift to me from her and her husband, Kurt.

Ted and Randy slept during the day. It was their escape. I was really worried about Ted. He barely talked, and he kept his emotions to himself. He was suffering from a bad back and was dealing with that pain too. He was scheduled to have back surgery that same week, but it had to be postponed. His surgery was rescheduled the week after Kelly's memorial service. The memorial was on a Saturday and was held at the church of St. Mary's in the mountains in Virginia City. Kelly's friend of many years, Melinda, said that Kelly and Darin had recently taken the four-wheelers up to Virginia City, and Kelly had come back excited and told Melinda she had just seen the most beautiful church.

Kelly's best friend, Shannon, and Shannon's mother-in-law made up a beautiful program and a picture poster that displayed the life of Kelly with her family, friends, and husband. Shannon was also the speaker at the memorial. When I first asked this of her, she said no. She was petrified in front of groups of people. She immediately then said yes. She knew that Kelly would help her through it. Thank you to Darin's fire chief and members of the fire department for all the plans, arrangements, and expenses.

Sunday, the day after the memorial, everyone went home. Randy and I were alone. We had to learn to live with this reality somehow. Monday, I felt the shock wearing off. It was so painful I could physically feel it. I felt like someone had beaten the daylights out of me. There wasn't a part of me that didn't ache. I wanted the shock back. I wanted it to ease away all my pains.

Tuesday morning, Randy and I headed to Meridian, Idaho, for Ted's back surgery. That same day, our daughter's obituary came out in our local newspaper. Randy drove, and when we got to the Bordertown (just before Reno), I asked Randy to let me drive. I needed to feel in control of something. I told him I would drive to Winnemucca, Nevada, then he could take over. Just on the other side of Reno was a mountain pass with curves, grades, and cliffs. All I saw was space. It was like I was driving through a blizzard (it was August) and a whiteout, and I didn't feel I was getting any traction. I had no reflexes. I wasn't in control. I had to pull over and let Randy drive. I had never felt so weak, so void, in all my life. The drive to Meridian felt like an eternity. We thought we would never get there. On that day, the reality set in. The helplessness and hopelessness was overwhelming. So many of the hopes and dreams Kelly had and we had for her were not to be fulfilled. They were gone. Her future was gone, and so was ours. Your children's future, their hopes and dreams, their children, your grandchildren—they are all part of you too. I wanted so desperately to jump out of the truck, but I knew that wasn't the answer. I wanted the pain to go away. It was tormenting me.

The things I have shared and expressed are a lot of the same feelings Randy, Ted, and Angel had too. Ted's surgery went well, and a week later, we headed home. I spoke daily on the phone with Angel, sometimes three times a day. Phone therapy. Ted still wasn't talking much. I just let him call me when he wanted or needed to. Our long-distance phone company called one night to inform me I was going to have a $600 phone bill. They wanted me to verify I was making the phone calls. This didn't surprise me, but they did put me on a better plan after learning what all the calls were about. That helped a whole lot.

In October, my sister Peggy told me that her husband, Kevin, had a week's vacation that month, and they wanted to take us anywhere we wanted to go. We wanted to see Ted and Angel. Their daughter Lacie, our sweet niece, came with us. They helped us through our pain. I am very close with my sister Peggy. There is a bond between us that can't be broken. I love all my siblings. We all share something different with each other.

My sister Adrienne also came that month. We weren't home when she arrived, so she went for a walk. She and her family live in San Jose, California, a good six-hour drive. When we got home, she approached us, and we could see she was crying. She hurt so bad for us. Adrienne is a very spiritual and compassionate person. She spent the week with us. She consoled us, and we consoled her. Another sister, Patty, was one of the first family members to arrive the day after the loss of Kelly, as she lives the closest. She went to buy all the food. She would not let us pay. She waited on guests, answered phones, and entertained our grandbabies. She did an unbelievable service for us.

My stepmom, Lloyd, was there to support and comfort us. You have to know this lady. She is a rock. I have always admired her strength.

Chapter Five

The Gifts

Bird Feather

Not long after our return trip home from Idaho, we got a phone call at three in the morning. I answered the phone. It was Ted. I could hear the anxiety in his voice as he apologized for the hour. He tried to wait for morning. I asked what was wrong, and he said, "I just had to hear your voice." We had all had a lot of nightmares and daymares. He didn't offer what it was about, and I didn't ask. We talked until 7:00 a.m. After our conversation, I went out back to sit and have a cup of coffee. I was awake now. We had a covered deck area out our sliding door, with the usual patio furniture. I sat on the chair closest to the door, staring into space in the direction of our trees out back. The overhang had wide eaves. Out of the corner of my eye, I caught something falling from underneath the eaves. What landed right in front of me was a tiny bird feather.

A few weeks before August 13, I shared with Kelly that my two baby birds, which were in a birdhouse under the eaves, had died. I love the baby swallows we get every year. Anyway, I was so sad, and she said, "Oh, Mom, I am so sorry. I know how much you love your birds." We had an unusually hot summer in 2003. This birdhouse had been purchased some years back, more as a decoration. No birds had ever nested in it before. We had other birdhouses out back for them. This birdhouse was made out of old barnwood, I am guessing, and had an old metal roof. I believe it got so hot inside, because of the metal roof, that the birds kept coming out onto the narrow ledge. I had placed lawn chairs with bed pillows underneath the birdhouse in case they'd fall out.

The first one did, and I discovered it had died. The second one started to fall (it was upside down), but Randy caught it. He put it back in its house. We knew that little bird would be abandoned because of what we did. I watched all day. Sure enough, Mom and Dad did not return. We were having a light rain outside. I got a flashlight and went to check on the baby bird, but he was gone. I looked everywhere—under shrubs, the deck, rocks, etc. During my search, I said to myself, "I have to save God's little creature." This verse from the Bible came to my mind: "Look how much I will do for the birds, do you not see how much more I will do for you?" I went back to the birdhouse, and searching with a drinking straw, I discovered the bird was buried under the nest of feathers. He had died also. I took down that birdhouse and threw it away. I didn't want that to ever happen again. That bird feather I spoke of earlier came down directly from where that birdhouse was. There was nothing up there but the reminder of it.

Rufus

I hope you can follow me with this story. Back in 1994, as if things weren't bad enough, our pump went out, and we had to hire a pumpman. Randy was suffering from a sinus infection, so he was unable to do it himself. Cameron, the pumpman, came and replaced our pump. Cameron's wife was Sherri, and she had a Christmas shop in her home called the Christmas Attic. I went there one day with my friend Nancy. I spotted a cute stuffed bear I wanted to get Kelly for Christmas. She loved all bears. Wolves were her spiritual animal, but she sure loved bears too. Well, the bear's name was Rufus. During this time, I was babysitting my little nephew Jesse, aged three, and he sure loved Rufus. One day, when Jesse was real sick, all he wanted was Rufus. Kelly let Jesse take Rufus home with him until he felt better. The following year, Kelly and I were on a mission to get Jesse his own Rufus. We found an identical Rufus (same color of ribbon and everything) at the Christmas

Attic once again. We wrapped the little bear in a shoe box and put it under the Christmas tree. When Jesse opened it on Christmas day and he saw Rufus in there, he said, "Rufus, what are you doing in there?" He had his own Rufus. After Kelly's passing, we gave Kelly's Rufus to my brother Larry and sister-in-law Debbie. They did so much of the painful stuff for us. We hoped Rufus would comfort them like he did their son Jesse.

Remember that I had lost my dear friend Nancy in 2001 and her husband, Mike, in 1999? Cameron and Sherri took over Crossroads Ministries, which Mike and Nancy had started. Shortly after August 13, 2003, Randy and I were on a return trip home from Reno, and I was on my cell phone with Angel. In the midst of our conversation, I no longer was talking with Angel but was interrupted by a gentleman.

He said, "Who are you?"

I said, "Just a mother trying to talk to her daughter. Who are you?"

"Just a guy trying to talk to his brother," he said. "Where you at?"

And I said, "On Highway 395 en route to Susanville."

He said he lived and was calling from Redding, California. "Maybe you know my brother and sister-in-law. They live in Susanville. Their names are Cameron and Sherri."

He was trying to talk with his brother at the same time I was trying to talk with Angel. I found this interesting. I think Nancy was letting me know Kelly was with her. Nancy had known Kelly from birth, and there was a special love between them. Kelly helped serve dinners occasionally at Crossroads.

There were numerous incidents that had taken place over time. They might not have been as intense in nature, some even very subtle, but nonetheless, they couldn't be ignored. In a conversation I had on the phone with my sister Peggy (as she set outside her home a few weeks after losing Kelly), she stated that everyone had gotten a butterfly but her. At almost that exact moment, she got her butterfly—an emotional moment. My brother and Angel were in our back bedroom talking about Kelly, and a picture of Kelly fell over.

Denielle, while writing cards to Ted and Angel by her open sliding door, had a bird feather blown in and land beside her. I can't tell you the countless times Angel and I would be talking on the phone (usually about Kelly) and the phone would go dead. One day, I was trying to share something with her about Kelly, and three times in a row this happened. I was getting a little annoyed, until Angel pointed out that she and Kelly had always shared how we were the power of three. We spoke another hour or so, and the phone did not die again.

I would find myself thinking about someone I hadn't thought about in a long time, and almost on cue, they would call. I would have a dream about something or someone, and it would come to pass. It was like someone knew my every thought. By themselves they seem insignificant, but together they are pretty powerful.

Evelyn

On the evening of December 1, 2003, the night before the preliminary hearing for an upcoming trial against the defendant, I had a phone conversation with Ted. In that conversation, he mentioned that he was surprised at how I could be so maternal, considering my mother lacked maternal instincts. I told him, "I believe you either are or you are not." I shared with him a story of a time I had walked home from school (approximately at the age of eight) with a girl named Tina. She invited me into her home and her mom, Evelyn, whom I had never met before, offered us a piece of chocolate cake and a glass of milk. They were served with loving-kindness. I remember thinking at that time that when I would grow up and have children, I would want to have a cake baked for them when they'd come home from school. It wasn't just the cake; it was what it was served with. Mind you, I didn't feel deprived of such things growing up. There were seven of us kids, and that's a lot of mouths to feed, so goodies were not a priority.

The point to the story is that I shared this with our son on December 1, and a week later, our local newspaper came out, and Randy told me that he had just read the obituaries. Evelyn, who no longer lived here in Susanville but in the Sacramento area, had died. I was on the phone with Angel at the time (again!) and told her about the Evelyn story I had shared with her brother the week before. Angel said, "Check the date of her passing." It was December 1, 2003, the same day I shared the story with Ted.

A short time after Kelly's crossing over, a lot of things started happening around us. One clock (battery operated) in particular kept losing and gaining time. Randy, who was not open to superstitions, kept saying the batteries were dying. I changed the batteries, but still, it always seemed to be off by twenty minutes. One morning, I was putting clothes in the dryer when it hit me to check another battery-operated clock in our family room. It had not been losing time, but that morning, it was off by twenty minutes. Randy still wasn't convinced. I bought a new clock. We went on vacation for a week, and the clock hadn't stopped but was off by four hours. Randy said, "Change the batteries." But I didn't. I didn't even touch it for a week. Never set the correct time. It didn't lose a minute. Over the next few months, the clock never lost a minute. Again I was gone for a week, and again, the clock was off by a few hours. I did change the batteries to appease Randy. He's a tough sale.

Kelly was with me a year before when I bought a large candle. I kept it wrapped in its cellophane and placed it in my bathroom. All of a sudden, I got this whiff of a beautiful fragrance. Nothing was in bloom; it was fall. I kept searching. I unwrapped the candle, and sure enough, the scent was coming from it. There was also the fragrance of Kelly's perfume. We had just bought it for her that last Christmas.

I told you what a tough sale Randy was. When I told him the story of my bird and the feather, he dissected the thing every which way. "Oh, it's probably this or it's probably that." Well, the first early spring afternoon in 2004, I was sitting out back in my usual spot when a small butterfly landed on the wall under our breezeway. Mind you, I had never seen a butterfly come into our covered breezeway before. I thought to myself, *I didn't get my first bird feather, but I got my first butterfly.* I went inside the house to read. I didn't share this with Randy. A few minutes later, Randy stepped outside, and about a foot out, he felt a *poof* (his word, not mine) of cold air on the back of his neck. He looked up, and a small (maybe a half-inch) bird feather fell from the covered ceiling. It landed right in front of him, onto a small woodpile.

He brought it in and said, "I have something for you." He opened his hand to reveal the feather.

I said, "Oh, that's not mine. That's yours. It came to you."

A few hours later, I picked up my *Better Homes and Gardens* magazine. On the front cover was a butterfly. It reminded me of the little one I had seen earlier and my thoughts at the time (about not getting a bird feather). I went in and shared the story with Randy and told him that was, in fact, my feather after all. There wasn't so much as a breeze that day, and his back was to the door. I loved hearing him convince me of this story. "The feather just fell from the ceiling!" He was not such a tough sell anymore!

Kindred Spirits

Just a few short days after Kelly's passing, friends Shannon and Melinda were over at Kelly and Darin's home when Shannon discovered a card with her name on it. Kelly must have set this card aside, intending on giving it to Shannon when she saw her next. Shannon opened it, and this is that card:

Shannon,

Wow! How can I express my gratitude for twelve years of friendship? I have always felt your love and support. You have been an honest friend in helping guide me when I did not know where I was going. You know me! You know who I am and what I stand for with no explanations needed. You have fought for me when I was unaware I needed to defend myself. Our friendship has been filled with love, and it is so easy to give even more. I cherish our friendship and appreciate how you have taught me a whole new way to live life. You are loved for the beaming light inside your soul, and this kindred spirit will be here for you for an eternity!

Love,
Kelly

> Shannon,
>
> Wow! How can I express my gratitude for twelve years of friendship. I have always felt your love and support. You have been an honest friend in helping guide me when I did not know where I was going. You know me! You know who I am, and what I stand for with no explanations needed. You have fought for me when I was unaware I needed to defend myself. Our friendship has been filled with love and it is so easy to give even more. I cherish our friendship and appreciate how you have taught me a whole new way to live life. You are loved for the beaming light inside of your soul and this kindred spirit will be here for you for an eternity!
>
> Love, Kelly

Smoke Detector

Every September, after the beginning of the school year, the elementary school our kids attended would have local fire trucks offer rides to the kids. Kelly really looked forward to these rides and the ice cream bars offered at the end of it. The street we live on is one of the main routes the trucks would take. On September 2004, I heard the sirens of the fire trucks as they passed our house. I stepped out back, and through my tears, I said, "Kelly, here come the fire trucks, honey. I know how much you loved them, and you grew up and married your fireman." These truck runs would last up to a couple of hours at times. In their last run of the night, on the last siren, our smoke detector went off. Randy and I looked at each other in bewilderment. At that exact moment, that exact time!

Our Song

There were songs that seemed to be sung for only us. One song in particular ("Here without You" by 3 Doors Down) would come on the moment I turned the radio in my car on. It was everywhere at the right time for all of us. Another one that played quite frequently on the airways was "Hole in the World" by the Eagles.

One day, as I got in my car to head to town, I turned on the radio and said, "Okay, God, what song are you going to play for me now?" The song "The Air that I Breathe" by the Hollies came on. I pulled off the road as I cried so hard. Kelly always told me I was the air that she breathed. Now, she is the air that I breathe.

Our dear friend Denielle (you will learn about her later in this book) and I were talking on the phone one night as we both watched the movie *The Five People You Meet in Heaven*. We had both recently read the book. She, being so young, did not know who the main actor, Jon Voight, was. She knew he was the father of Angelina Jolie but did not know him as an actor. She asked, "What movie is he best known for?" The movie that came to my mind was *Midnight Cowboy* from the 1970s. She had never seen it or heard of it. I asked if she had ever heard the song "Midnight Cowboy." No, she didn't think so. Well, I sang her the lyrics (poorly, I might add) to the song. The next day, as I headed to town, I turned on my radio, which was still on a Reno station from the trip before. Static came on, but I chose to wait until I could pick up the signal a block away. The static cleared, and the song "Midnight Cowboy" came on. I used to call things like these coincidences, but they were coming one after another for us. The harder it was to understand it, the more convinced we were that these things weren't just happening.

A Little Request

Now, here is something that surpasses all understanding. At six thirty one morning, we got a phone call. Randy was already up and in the kitchen, and I came flying out of bed because of the hour. It was a gentleman returning a call to us that he had received at 1:00 a.m. Mind you, he did not identify himself to Randy. Randy said that we did not call him or anyone else at such an hour. The man said that the phone rang at 1:00 a.m., and he and his wife did not answer it, but the caller

ID showed our home phone number. No, that wasn't us; we did not call them. Well, a shouting match developed (I could hear the caller getting upset with Randy, and Randy with him), so I signaled for Randy to give me the phone. I asked the gentleman if I could help him. He conveyed to me what he had told Randy. I said, "I'm sorry, sir, but no one from our home called you or anybody else at that hour." I told him it was only me and my husband at home, and nobody else could have called him from here. We were asleep at 1:00 a.m. We dissolved the conversation. It took Randy and me a while to shake it off.

Later that morning, I called Angel and shared with her about this call. Before we ended our conversation, I shared with her that at midnight the night before, I went to Kelly's picture (as I did every night before going to bed) and had my usual talk with her. I told her that we hadn't heard from her in a while and if she could give us a sign that she was still with us. Angel said, "What time was that?" I said midnight straight up (I had just looked at the clock). She said she had asked the same thing of Kelly at one o'clock her time. She lives in Idaho, and they were ahead of us by an hour. Okay, so we got the message out to Kelly.

I hung up on Angel, and a few minutes later, my phone rang. It was Mary, Angel's mother-in-law. Hmm. She had never called me before. We had a wonderful relationship and the common interest of our kids and grandkids, but we had never called each other.

Mary said, "Jan, that call you got this morning, it was from Gary," her husband.

I said, "What?"

She said the phone did ring at 1:00 a.m. Colorado time (ahead of us also by an hour), and the caller ID showed our phone number, but they didn't recognize it as ours. After the conversation Gary had with us, he went for a jog. I'm sure he had to shake it off too. He thought to himself, *It sure sounded like Janice, Angel's mom.* He returned home and told Mary this. She pulled out her Christmas card list, and sure enough, she saw that was our phone number.

Now, Mary is as sweet as they come, and it took no convincing her that we didn't make the call. We both tried to understand this. Gary got on the phone and was in good humor about it all. We called each other back a couple of times that day, still trying to figure it out. I shared with them the request to Kelly that Angel and I had made the night before at the exact same time. Gary was convinced that Kelly had called them.

I joked with him that I would have a talk with her about the hour. He replied, "That Kelly can call us anytime, day or night."

Four o'clock that afternoon, I felt I had to try to get to the bottom of how this could have happened. I called our local phone repairman at home; it was the weekend. We had known this man personally for years. I shared with him what I have shared with you. He said, "Jan, stranger things have happened that we can't explain." He explained how the phone system works today. It's all by computer. At one time, we would have had made a call to Gary and Mary from our home phone. Well, we never had, but Angel and their son Brian (while visiting us) had called from our home before. He said something about numbers being stored in the system, and something triggers the computer to let it know the call you want made. He said that something must have happened that night from our phone line for the call to have been made.

I asked if there could have been a glitch in the system. He said, "If there were, we would have a messed-up system." The thing that was so puzzling to me was that of all the hundreds of calls to my kids' family and friends, why Gary and Mary's? Few calls had ever been made to them from our number. Maybe the other ones would have been too obvious. It would be months later, in a conversation I had with both Gary and Mary (we were at our grandson Liam's first birthday party in Boise), they shared with me that that call they had received from us at 1:00 a.m. was not the first call from our number. It was the third call, and they were all after the midnight hour. Gary said that was what got his attention. We kept calling them at this not-so-decent hour. I would be making a phone call too. Anyway, the phone calls have stopped.

The Grandpa Story

Frank (father-in-law), after having gall bladder surgery, then later suffering a heart attack while in the hospital where the doctors had to revive him, shared with us that he had seen some of his family and friends who had passed on. One of these friends would be Ardelle. Ardelle passed away while Frank was in the hospital. He had no knowledge of his passing. Before his own passing, he spoke mostly of family and friends way back to his childhood. He was not in the here and now. When he saw me, he called me Leta, his sister-in-law. He did not know who Randy was. One time, he even called me Santa Claus.

The last time I spent with Frank in the hospital, he asked me what all the lights were outside his window. I told him it was the lights of Reno. He was on the fifth floor of the hospital, and unless you were standing at the window, looking down, you wouldn't see the lights. I laid my head next to his and looked out the window, and I couldn't see the lights of Reno. I think these were different lights he was asking about. Grandson Ted went and spent his last night with his grandpa at the hospital. He slept in a chair next to his best friend. The nurses said that whenever Frank became upset or combative, Ted was always able to calm him down. He knew he was in the company of someone he loved very much.

A Sense of Kelly

Brian, while at Darin and Kelly's home to meet Denielle for the first time, had an experience of his own. He was taking out the garbage to the curb when he got a whiff of Kelly's perfume. He kept on getting that scent he was familiar with. He even looked through some of the garbage to find out where it was coming from. He was outside for a long time. He shared this with Angel much later.

Another time, he went to his local Home Depot for some supplies. Upon entering Home Depot, he glanced over at a tall blonde girl looking at some flowers outside, and she smiled at him. He swore it was Kelly. She went inside the nursery, and Brian continued into the store. Before continuing in search of the items he wanted to purchase, he had to go back outside to see if he could find the girl. She was gone. He was so shaken by the possibility of having just seen Kelly that he went home without making a purchase.

I Thought of You

A few months after August 13, I thought of a lady I had worked with for nineteen years at the supermarket. Her name was Carolyn, and while we got along nicely at work, we never socialized together. She never called me at home (except once to ask me a question), nor had I called her. I really liked Carolyn but had never really had the habit of thinking about her like I did that morning. What I got was a phone call from her. I told her to hold on a moment—I had to compose myself. I told her that I had been thinking about her all morning, and she said it was like someone was nudging her to call me. We spoke of the obvious concerns of the time, and she wanted to end our conversation with a prayer. She prayed for me and my family the most beautiful prayer I had ever heard. It was quite lengthy, but I know I didn't want it to end. She really helped me with her words of healing. God bless you, Carolyn, for the call and the prayer.

Niagara Falls

Just this past winter, I had awoken and was heading to the kitchen when I heard water running in the utility room. I was barefoot and expected floodwater everywhere. We had been experiencing freezing temperatures and thought the running water was from a broken pipe. The floor was dry, and I inspected the pipes behind the washer. It sounded like Niagara Falls! Where was all the water coming from? I then opened the lid to the washer and discovered a drumful of water, and it was still filling up. The washer was empty of laundry, so it was really loud as it was filling up. You had to push on a knob, turn to cycle, then pull out the knob to start it. There were also a series of customized cycle buttons you could select from, and one of those was an extra rinse button. Just by pushing on this button, the drum would fill for extra rinse. The washer was fairly new and did not have any problems before or since that morning. What in the world?

I Want to Know

I have always been open to happenings, and yes, I was desperate to know that Kelly's life did not end. Here, yes, but that she is somewhere and is happy. Maybe in Italy, seeing the Roman ruins that she loved so much. I was searching, but I was not reaching for an answer. That was the beautiful thing about all this. It was real and at times exciting. Maybe it was the hope of it for all of us. As Angel and I would often say to each other, "We are 95 percent sure there is a heaven, but there is that 5 percent of doubt." This shows our shaky faith. Can God maybe pull back the curtains and just let us have a peek at Kelly? We want to see that she is happy and hanging out and fishing with Grandpa. Can

AN EARLY LIGHT

we just have that glimpse? That 95 percent is a pretty good percentage, but that 5 percent is grueling.

Occasionally I would watch programs with mediums and, like so many others, would have a fascination about the process. We all want to believe, and when you lose a loved one, it goes from belief to a need for certainty. One of the questions asked so often of a medium is, why do some loved ones come through for family and friends, and some don't? There really is no direct answer because they don't know for sure, only suppose. I have asked many times, "Why is this happening to us? Why are so many signs presented to us?" Even when I was cursing God, he kept blessing us. He must not have taken it personally. I often wonder if anger isn't love turned inside out.

Angel, Kelly, and I would at times discuss these programs we had watched or a book we might have read pertaining to the afterlife. We three would share how we would do everything we could to come through for the other ones. I know we discussed how we would do this, but these gifts we were getting, we never discussed. Most of these experiences I've shared with you came quickly the weeks and months after August 13. As time went on, they became less frequent and soon happened only on occasion! This is how I feel about the intensity and duration of them.

From the get-go, we all had such a need for an affirmation that Kelly's life continued on. We could handle this and we could survive this if it didn't just end for her. As we came to recognize and accept that these circumstances surrounding us weren't just coincidental, we became comforted by them. God was comforting us by allowing Kelly to come through for us. He knew how desperately we needed to know. For a long time, this was one of those big whys I had. I guess I couldn't figure out why we were being both punished and blessed at the same time. I came to believe then that this wasn't a punishment for Kelly or us. Why is it that the bad stuff is easier to believe than the good stuff? We had to believe in the good—the bad just didn't make sense!

By request, I have had to omit a few stories that are so beautiful in order to protect the innocent and innocence of them, again showing us how God is working in our lives for the good.

Our daughter-in-law did not want her children, our grandchildren, to be part of this, so I had to exclude some stories (beautiful ones) and their names to honor her wishes. She lived this and was resentful how it affected our lives. Yeah, it was one big painful party for all of us, one I wish we weren't invited to. Even the beautiful parts would make you cry.

I believe that had we not pulled together in this or saw God's hand in it, we would have wandered aimlessly through it. There were times I couldn't tell if we were getting better or just used to the pain. You don't ever want to get used to that pain. You want to find that light at the end of the tunnel, the pot of gold at the end of a rainbow. That is where the hope and riches are.

Chapter Six

A Million Thoughts

The Dead Lawn

Some years back, a couple had lost their daughter while she was in her teens. When my children were little, I loved taking them to their house for Halloween, as the father really got into the ghosts and goblins for the children. They had a beautiful yard, which was beautifully decorated during the Christmas holidays. After the loss of their daughter, their lawn died. No more ghosts and goblins, and lights were out at Christmas. I remember saying to Randy days later after the thirteenth, as I saw our own lawn dying, "Please don't let the lawn die." Yes, the lights were up for the holidays, not for us but for our neighbors. I was so saddened to see everything stop for that family. I didn't want others to suffer that way. I guess it was my way of telling them that we were okay.

As time went on, I got back into the routine of some household chores. I was doing okay this one day, or so I thought, when I felt something wet on my cheek. I was crying. I didn't even know I was crying.

I finally got brave enough to go to our family physician six months later for my yearly exam. I broke down in the examination room, and the doctor said, "I think you need help." He ordered a chemical panel and prescribed me with an anxiolytic or an antidepressant. It took me away from the pain and helped me to be me again. This was in February. March was my birthday, and my sister Peggy, who lives in Sacramento, wanted to meet me in Reno and go gamble and have some fun. What did I have to lose?

She was coming over with her husband, Kevin, who had business in Reno, and we would all go to dinner and gamble. I found a slot machine called the Titanic. The aim of the game was to keep the ship from sinking. The first twenty dollars I put in were for Kelly. The slot machine took it all. The second twenty dollars were for Angel. I won one hundred dollars, cashed it in, and tucked it away in my wallet. I put in twenty dollars more and lost. Peggy, Kevin, and I headed to our rooms. Peggy was staying with me as Kevin had to sleep for work. I really wanted to save the Titanic, so Peggy and I snuck out and found our slot machine. We took turns trying to keep the Titanic from sinking. It was a weeknight, so there were not a lot of big-time gamblers. We pretty much had the place to ourselves. The machine was teasing us, and we fell for it hook, line, and sinker—no pun intended.

Around two o'clock in the morning, we both felt like having a glass of milk (we were not drinking). This sweet elderly man came around and asked if we would like a drink. We said, "Is there any way we can get a glass of milk?" He obliged. We continued to gamble and drink milk; we got refills. The Titanic sank, and we were broke. Peggy asked if I had any money left, and I said, "No, except for Angel's hundred-dollar bill."

Peggy said, "Nah, we couldn't."

I agreed and then said, "The heck we can't! If we are going down, she's going down with us." We cashed it in and gambled some more, and our ship went down.

We headed to our room, and a few casino attendants (who we were sure were watching us and knew we were a couple of fools) said good night. On the way to the room, I told Peggy that when the morning shift comes on, I was sure they were going to ask how it was the night before. Their fellow workers would respond with "Oh, there were a couple of ladies trying to keep the Titanic from sinking until four o'clock in the morning."

"What were they drinking?"

"Milk!"

We laughed all the way to our room. I threw myself on the bed in laughter. Then I heard myself. I said, "Peggy, do you hear me? I am laughing." It was the first time I had heard myself laugh since losing Kelly. Thank you, Peggy. By the way, Angel said, "The hundred dollars was the best investment ever."

I never imagined I would ever find laughter or humor in anything again. Life was not funny. If somebody told me back on August 13 that I would laugh again to find joy in my days, I would have bet plenty they would be wrong. I wanted to just curl up and die. I knew my life would be so full of hate and anger, sorrow and pain. There was no escaping it.

Someone had offered me not long after our loss that everything was happening for the glory of God. I couldn't have cared less. I had this internal argument going on with God—like I thought I could win that one! I hated that I couldn't turn to him for comfort and strength; I always had before. You talk about feeling alone. There is nothing more frightening than believing that God is not only punishing you but abandoning you as well. He didn't abandon me, but I did. It would be months before I would come back to God in prayer. I would usually just say the Lord's Prayer. I didn't know how to pray anymore. I didn't feel my prayer for Kelly was answered. It would be around this time that I would turn all this over to God. I had been asking the big *whys* of this, looking at it from all angles to try to figure it out. I stopped, looked up, and said, "I surrender this all to you, God." I was finished.

Randy and I spent the winter in our bedroom. We ate most of our meals in bed. We would get up and do what had to be done for the day but soon return to our room. It was our comfort zone. We grew to hate our home. What was once warm and comforting became dark and depressing. I even, at one time, wanted to burn it down. I didn't, something I am sure our insurance company was grateful for. I know, I would have only hurt myself—an arsonist. I wanted to destroy everything. It was like I wanted to prove to God that nothing mattered to me. I was still bargaining. We tried rearranging the home, but that didn't help, so we pretty much gutted it. Now that was better; no furniture to sit on, but we felt better. I had a conversation some weeks later with Ted and told him how I felt. He said my life had been destroyed. My life and environment had changed, and I needed to change with it. I don't know why I didn't figure that out for myself.

Angel came down from Idaho, and we started rebuilding our environment. We headed to Robbins House of Furniture. We spent a solid week going through catalogs, matching fabrics and decor. I was inspired by Kelly to go Venetian. She, Ted and Angel as well, loved their Italian heritage. We spent so much time down at Robbins House of Furniture that at one time, Al, the owner, greeted Angel and me with a time card. Months later, Al even offered me a job. Oh dear god, I was afraid of that. I wasn't ready for the public. Al and his wife, Joy, are wonderful people, and whether they know it or not, they have helped me through a difficult time. What a great sense of humor they both have. I was doing normal stuff again and felt among the living. There were times I would be in there, laughing with them—as well as Nancy, an employee—go get in my vehicle, and cry all the way home. After buying the furniture, I looked for the final decor needed to bring it all together.

I had been looking for some Italian-looking sconces and had pretty much lived down at Robbins, but they did not have what I was looking for. I had gone to Boise and even looked there, but no luck. The day after my weeklong stay in Boise, I kept getting this urge to go back to Robbins and search again for those sconces. I was having this argument with myself that I had covered the whole store and they weren't to be found. I was tired, jet-lagged, and just not in the mood. The urge persisted. I threw myself together and headed to Robbins. I walked in, and right in front of me, sitting on top of the console I had just purchased, were the sconces I had been looking for. Robbins had just got them in. Hmm. Thank you, Al, Joy, and Nancy.

There were so many changes taking place in all of us. The concerns of depression, anxiety, panic, and high blood pressure. We were dealing with so many pains. One was going to the doctor for this and another for that. Thank goodness the help was there.

I became less tolerant of people and things. I didn't want to take this out on anyone; they didn't do this to me. My heart was grieving for Kelly, and I had no room for any more grief, not even the grief of my past. I had to get rid of it and dump it back where it belonged. I had said for years that I would take these pains with me to my grave. If I shared my hurts, I would be hurting those I had struggled for years to have a relationship with.

I wasn't so eager to share all these happenings with anyone but a few family and friends. I was so afraid that people would question the validity of them. I was so worried about what people would think or say, until one day, after one of these stories I had shared with you (it was the "Midnight Cowboy" song I heard on the car radio), I made a promise to Kelly that I would never question these gifts. I told Randy then that I don't care what people think or say. These are too beautiful to keep to myself. It doesn't matter if some don't believe they are real or not. I know they are, and I have been too comforted and excited not to share them. Besides, I can't glorify God if I keep them to myself. I don't deserve the credit—he does. I believe that most people want to believe in God, and I think how when a person is faced with fear or death, they cry out to God—"Help me, God," "Dear God," "My God," "Forgive me, God." We believe!

I can't say that I set out to write a book, even though I was encouraged by many. I had all these thoughts and feelings inside me, and one day I guess they just had to get out. I felt like I was going to explode if I didn't free myself of them.

I woke up one Saturday morning in early September 2005, and I had a thought (one of about a million) and felt like I needed to write it down. It was the introduction. It was 11:00 a.m., and I was still in my pajamas and felt like I needed to get busy with my day. I had another thought, so I wrote it down. I never did get dressed that day; the thoughts just kept on coming. I wrote until 3:00 a.m. I was becoming delirious with fatigue (those writings I did omit), so I shut it down for the night. I woke up a few hours later and kept on writing. Over the next two weeks, I took my tablet with me everywhere I went. I had another thought . . . while I was cooking dinner, mopping, etc.

I kept on writing. I literally wrote nonstop for two weeks, until there was nothing more to say. For the first time in over two years, my mind was quiet. It felt so good to get it all out and to just rest. I do have to admit that I felt I needed to document some things so as to not forget them. I had, during this time, been jotting events down, but those were just a few one-liners. This was a little different. I was sleep deprived, suffering with bloody knuckles and inflamed shoulder blades, but I had another thought. One thing I did not suffer from was writer's block. I almost prayed for it. What a relief when I was done. This was intended for only us.

Originally, what I wrote was the heart of this, but as time went on, I felt like I needed to add substance, share more history, stuff like that. English and grammar weren't my strong points in school, so I had to do a little homework too! I really did struggle in school. One thing I did have was happiness and a sense of humor. How do you go through something like this, as well as write a book as serious in nature as this, and still maintain these qualities?

I wanted to die with Kelly, but God wasn't going to let me. If I'd lose the happiness and my sense of humor, my hope, and my joy, if I couldn't find the peace, I would be dead. Dead in faith and spirit and dead to a God I love. He didn't let that happen. That isn't death; that is dying.

I haven't experienced these afterlife communications from all family and friends who have passed on. I always hoped for a sign but didn't receive one. I don't know how this works. Maybe it's all in good time. After I lost my friend Nancy, I hoped for anything to let me know she was still here with us. She chose to wait a couple of years, until we lost Kelly, to let me know. She let me know in the biggest way.

After I lost my father-in-law, Frank, in 2000, I got what I will call a visit to let me know he was still with us. It came months after his passing. I had just rolled over one night to get in my sleeping position when I felt someone pressing on my upper back. I didn't move and was afraid to look up. When I did look up, no one was there. I was home alone that night, so I got up and searched the house to see if someone was inside. I looked under beds, closets, everywhere someone could hide. I even doubled back, thinking someone might be trying to trick me. No one was in the house. I did not know what that was about!

Dorothy (my mother-in-law) shared with me a dream she had had about Frank around the same time. It got me thinking about the last thing I had done for Frank the last time I had spent with him just before he went into the hospital, and it was rubbing his shoulder blades. I had gone over to his house to see how he was doing—not good. He was so frail, weak, and his shoulder blades were hurting.

He said, "Jan, my shoulder blades are killing me."

I said, "Roll over, Grandpa." I always called him Grandpa—and he loved it—and I went to get him some ointment, crawled into bed beside him, and rubbed his shoulder blades.

The next morning, before he headed to Reno with Ted for a doctor's appointment, he sat in his chair in and out of consciousness. He woke up when I came in the house, lifted his head, and said, "Thank you for the back rub." His head went back down. He never came home from that doctor's appointment. In fact, they had to call for an ambulance from their clinic. Grandpa barely had a pulse, and his blood pressure was so low they couldn't believe this man had walked on his own strength. We lost him a short time later.

I don't know if it was Grandpa in the room with me that night, but it does make sense. If I dismiss the possibility, then I will have missed the gift. That was my one and only from Grandpa.

Chapter Seven

The Painful Journey

Before you go further into this book, I want you to know that I prayed along the way for God's guidance in this. I have tried to put things chronologically so as not to sound contradictory. These happenings are true and factual, with no exaggerations. They are inspirational and intended to comfort and heal you, the reader. I know that someday I am going to stand before God, and I don't want to have to answer for any deception on this project.

This is a compilation of thoughts, feelings, and events written on whatever I could find to write them on. It is the patchwork of our lives since losing Kelly. I have tried to put them together so the narrative flows without hesitation. I wasn't always able to accomplish that, but I worked it in anyway because it is part of the fabric.

It has been a long and painful journey living and writing it. I've cried along the way, but I've also laughed and seen for myself the growth that has taken place in all of us. There were times I felt I was inspired with some of my writings. All I know is that I felt like I had to keep the pen moving. I knew I was writing this for someone. Maybe it's you.

Just recently, I was told by a friend that someone had commented on how happy Randy and I appear to be. I am sure a lot of people have wondered this themselves. Sometimes I have even asked myself how I can be happy about anything. We have the faith, the gifts, and the guidance needed to travel through this. We do not want to be down all the time and depressing for the people around us. We are real in the presence of others, and we want to be someone they want to keep company with. We just choose to keep our grieving in private.

One morning (in December 2004), after Randy came home from work, he announced he was having chest pains and had been all night. It hurt to take deep breaths. Panic set in. We went to the hospital. They ran all the usual tests on him to rule out a heart attack. As I sat in the waiting room, I had the usual daymares. How would I tell Ted and Angel they had lost their father? How would I pull through? You might as well dig a hole for all of us. All the tests came back fine. The doctor was still examining him when I remembered, the day before, Randy had been sick to his stomach and spent most of the day vomiting (sorry). Could he have maybe pulled a muscle? The doctor said absolutely, and it appeared that's what had happened. A few days later, the pain was gone.

Fear, anxiety, and panic—everything around us had heightened. We were held hostage by the fear, so much to overcome. The court stuff dragged on and on and on. You know how it goes. It's not easy to find a guilty man guilty.

The delay for Clyde's arrest had to do with how his blood was obtained in the hospital that night. The i's were dotted and the t's were crossed, and on October 30, 2003, a warrant was issued for his arrest. He turned himself in. He posted bail and was free to continue the same lifestyle. We were going to trial. We were going to be able to fight for Kelly, fight for justice. We promised her that!

I have to leave out a whole lot of what I know because I don't want another lawyer in my life! Clyde's father was a retired professor of law and lawyer/judge himself. We knew what we were up against. This was someone who knew the law. He learned it, he taught it, and in our opinion, he was now using it. How do we go up against that? We knew we were in for a long fight, and it was.

We had many conversations over the course of time with the DA. Not one time in an almost two-year battle did they not ever take my call. I was always put through. The lady from the crisis center was a godsend. The investigator grew up in Westwood, a small town thirteen miles west of Susanville. As it turned out, he and Randy went to elementary school together. They didn't know each other, but it was still a coincidence. Our lawyer had the same birthday as our Kelly. He caught that right off the bat.

Early on, after we found out who Clyde's father was and after the warrant was issued, we learned of a declaration that was made by Clyde during the booking. What he said sent a girl from court services away, crying, and someone else had to take over for her. If I told you what he had said, it would be hearsay, and I would be in trouble. Anyway, my heart was racing all the time. I had to accept then and there that I had to get a grip or I would not see this through to trial. I wanted more than anything to fight for Kelly.

A calm came over me. I had to trust that the truth would be made known and the scales of justice would prevail. It was amazing—I found myself feeling relaxed about it even. Even though I was mad at him, deep down I knew that God had it under control. I wasn't visualizing this! (I don't feel that is going to happen!) It's all going to be fine. That was pretty much the attitude I'd adopted during the course of all this. It had all worked out the way I saw it would. I would have wasted so much time getting worked up over something I couldn't control.

You wouldn't believe the calendar of events that we had gone through. We were constantly landing on and dodging dates. The *Lassen County Times* called me on November 18 for a newspaper interview, on Kelly's birthday. One court date, Ted's birthday, was cancelled. The trial was to start on July 20, Randy's birthday. That was delayed and rescheduled for the week of November 18, again Kelly's birthday. That too was delayed because of health issues for Clyde.

At the beginning of all this, Clyde had to turn over his driver's license and passport and be drug-tested on a regular basis. Since Kelly worked at the court services in Washoe County, he had to be drug-tested elsewhere. Court services at the Washoe County Courthouse wouldn't or couldn't because of conflict of interest.

In January 2005, the judge that had been overseeing the case went on to become the superior court judge. We were assigned a new judge. A new date was set for the beginning of the year. Guess who became judge and was assigned our case? None other than our lawyer. Obviously, he had to recuse himself. Great, another postponement! We had to be assigned a new judge! He seemed to be on top of this case. We were really impressed with him. He ordered a copy of the drug test results. There weren't any. Clyde had not been tested all this time. He was drug-tested the next morning, and he failed. He was put in jail and remained there until sentencing. There was no trial. The blood evidence was not thrown out, and Clyde pleaded guilty.

On the day of sentencing, family and friends had the opportunity to speak on behalf of Kelly. I read the essay "From Innocence to Experience," which she had written, and also the letter she had written to Randy and me, which we received shortly after her wedding day. I believe her own words were more powerful than any other's. The judge gave Clyde the maximum sentence of twenty years. We *got* him, Kelly! We *got* him off the streets! We *got* justice for you, baby! Thank you, Washoe County. Thank you, God!

Chapter Eight

Dragon Lady

My mother-in-law, Dorothy, lives *right next door* to us. Randy and his parents bought the lots where we now live back when Randy was sixteen. Before we started plans for our home, we made sure they did *not* want to build on their lot. They had just bought a home in Susanville the year before. They had bought the lot only as an investment. No, they would not be building next to us.

A year after we moved into our new home, my mother-in-law shared their wishes to make their newest home *right next door*! Dorothy and my father-in-law, Frank, asked permission to move one hundred feet away from us. Now, Frank was as harmless as they come. Dorothy, however . . . well, have you seen *Everybody Loves Raymond*? Dorothy is my Marie!

Now, how do I stand before my mother-in-law of a few years and say no? Everybody who knows Dorothy, and most everyone does, knows what I am talking about. I was told to speak now or forever hold my peace. I told her I'd help her pick out her linoleum. I have been forever holding my peace! Now I too owned a lot!

I had my children lie for me at an early age: "If Grandma asks what you had for dinner, don't tell her you had hotdogs. Tell her you had steak and lobster and broccoli." It wasn't all that bad! We grew to have an understanding of each other: you stay over there, and I will stay over here. Dorothy means well. She is very loving of her family and very protective. She is not afraid to go up against anyone. All this is used by permission of Dorothy. She would be the first one to sue me.

There were many perks. We have come a long way together! I used to be afraid of her. Thirty-five long years later, she is afraid of me. The first time she told me that, I said, "You have got to be kidding. Afraid of me? Yeah."

I learned my ABCs in school, but I learned my Ws from Dorothy—*who*, *what*, *when*, *where*, and *why*. Our kids learned to come clean with Mom and Dad as to what they did over the weekend because they knew Grandma would learn all about their goings-on by Monday morning and share the knowledge with Randy and me. I don't know how she does it, but Dorothy knows most everything about most everybody. She is like a radar.

If she would come in through my back door, then I could see her coming. I could see her coming a hundred feet away. You could set music to it (a drumroll, maybe), to her approach, and it allowed me time to do some breathing exercises. However, if she'd approach from the front entrance, there would be no warning!

One day, she really caught me off guard, and I have to admit, I would have loved a video of it. I remember having a towel on my head, so you know I wasn't ready for my day yet. I was getting the whole Ws regimen, and I don't know what came over me, but the next thing I knew, I was jumping up and down on the couch, screaming, "What do you want me to do about it?" Then I went up on the arm of it before my dismount. She looked at me and said, "You need help!" No truer statement! God, love her—if I'd ever decide to write a poem about her, I can promise it would be most entertaining, twenty-nine years (living next door) worth. Once in awhile, I still mumble to myself, "I do believe my mother-in-law told me to stick cheese up my butt!" She has threatened to move for years, and we've offered to help any way we could, but now, why bother? We want to keep her around for the sheer entertainment.

Just yesterday, she called to tell me that she just found out that if she'd live to be one hundred, she wouldn't collect on her insurance. "Oh lord of my rocking boat."

She lost Frank a few years before Kelly. He passed on April 15, 2000. Death and taxes. We thought he would find the humor in that. After we lost Frank, I couldn't cry. I don't know why. I dearly loved the man. I can still see him walk in the back door and ask, "Jan, do you have any sweets?" He was borderline diabetic, so he did not have the privilege of sweets. A month after his passing, the floodgates opened for me. I wrote this poem about him:

A Poem for Grandpa

Grandpa left us a month ago
We were so sad—we loved him so
God gave him eighty years
A wonderful life, so why the tears
We didn't want to let him go
For selfish reasons, you have to know
He was delightful and funny
Not a day went by
That he didn't make you laugh
Till you had tears in your eyes
A story he could tell
From dusk till dawn
Just ask Ted, his buddy, grandson
He worked so hard all his life
To bring comfort for his family and wife
Friends, oh, he had plenty
His life was full, never empty
Golfing and fishing he shared with some
But hunting he did with his son
A beautiful garden
His fruits and labors
He shared with us and all the neighbors
I am sure he had many pets
But Josie and Tracy I'll never forget
He loved them like you and me
They weren't dogs—they were family
I remember him fondly every day
And once in a while he'll hear me say
"You were the bravest man I've ever known
You walked till the end, onto the throne
I want to leave this world, you see
With that much love known to me"

AN EARLY LIGHT

I had never seen Dorothy cry so long and so hard as she did over Kelly. My heart broke for her. Keep in mind these kids were over Grandma and Grandpa's house as much as ours. Months had gone by when one day, Dorothy came over, crying, and said, "One day, I want to be with Kelly and Frank again, but I don't think God's going to let me in."

I said, "Dorothy, you just have to quit being so ornery. Every day, when you get up, consider God in all that you think, say, and do. Watch Joel Osteen on television from Lakewood Church in Houston, Texas."

One night, around eleven thirty (way past Dorothy's bedtime, not mine), she called to tell me she had just watched Joel. She said, "He was talking about me!" He was talking about all of us, but she felt he was directing his sermon at her. I also had been watching him that night and remember thinking, *I sure hope Dorothy is hearing this.* Joel's sermon was called "Are you making a deposit in life or a withdrawal?" I needed it too! I get a kick now when Dorothy says, "Did you watch Joel on Sunday?"

Upon a return trip home from Reno a few weeks after Kelly's memorial, we received a sympathy card that brought with it comfort that was insurmountable.

I walked in the house, and Randy said, "We got a card today from a girl named Denielle." She said she was with Kelly the night of the accident. I was shaking so bad I could hardly hold the card. This was her letter to us:

Dear Janice and Randy,

I am so sorry I didn't get to meet you when you came to Reno. Thank you so much for the beautiful angel. I have her on my bedroom shelf, looking over at the wedding picture of Darin and your beautiful daughter. I am so sorry for your loss. I don't exactly know the words to comfort your hearts, but I do need you to know that Kelly was not alone. I stayed by her side until they made me stand back, but I was the last person to leave that night aside from the police. I don't know if Darin told you, but the day after, I had this urge to get a charm bracelet (Nomination), and an angel charm jumped at me. I was told this was special to Kelly. I also wanted you to know, that evening, I felt Kelly there, which was extremely overwhelming because I didn't know her. She will always be in my heart and as will the entire family, the Tassis and the Berrys.

*All my love,
Denielle Capozzi*

Kelly wasn't alone! Oh, dear God, she wasn't alone. Denielle lived in North Reno, and she was visiting her mom and grandmother in South Reno. They lived on the corner of Gold Run and Toll Road. Denielle was in her car, getting ready to head for home, when her mom detained her by telling her a joke. If she hadn't, Denielle might have been at the corner herself as the truck carrying our Kelly passed through. Randy and I had learned from Darin of the help this young girl and her mother had offered Kelly and Darin that night. That was why we gave the angel gifts and pictures.

* * *

Here's Denielle's account of that night:

Have You Ever Known Someone Before You've Met Them?

After I had dispatched for the highway patrol, death became a huge part of my life. I became almost numb to it. If you separate yourself from the fact that these fatalities were real people with real families, you won't hurt. All that changed the evening of August 13, 2003. I had been out visiting my family and decided to head home (it was a little after 8:00 p.m.). I was in my car, ready to turn the key, when my mom came out the front door with the family dog. She was acting silly to get my attention, so I got out of the car to chat for a minute. Not two minutes later, I heard something I had never heard before, but I identified it immediately. My mom and I looked up and saw a huge cloud of dust. The silver Toyota emerged from the confusion and came to rest on the curb of the corner, just in front of the streetlight. We ran to the sidewalk to see what had happened when we saw this man staggering out of his truck. He turned away from his vehicle and started in our direction. My mom went to him, and I ran into her house to call 911. At this point, I didn't have all the details of the accident, but I knew we needed medical attention immediately. I told the dispatcher what my mom had yelled to me as I ran for the phone, "I see a bike! Someone was hit!"

After hanging up the phone, I ran back up to the truck. When I walked around the back end of the truck, I saw her. A young woman had been hit. One of the neighbors at the scene was a nurse; she knelt down alongside her lifeless body. Everything went into slow motion. I felt a warmth; I felt a life. The strange part about that was that this life was beside me, not inside this woman's body, where it belonged. It was at that moment that I knew she would be a part of me for the rest of my life.

I decided that too much time was passing, and no one had shown up yet to take care of this woman that I had become so protective over. I ran back to the house. I called a trooper that I had known from highway patrol—he just lived down the street. He was at the corner before I even made it around the corner. When I walked out the front door to go back to the corner, my grandma stopped me. "Why are you going back?" I looked at her as if she were speaking a foreign language, and before I had time to think of what to say, I blurted out, "If that were me, I wouldn't want to be alone." I would later know that those words had much more meaning than I had realized at that time.

I knelt down beside her twisted body. To this day, I still can't remember for sure if I touched her leg, but I remember wondering, *Where are her shoes?* I looked up and down the street. *Where did all these people come from?* I started to feel angry. I was on a mission to protect this stranger. I wanted to scream at the top of my lungs, "Go home! Stop staring!" I looked up and saw more people behind my mom's backyard fence (which ran along the road where the accident had happened). There had been another person hit. How the man and woman were related, if at all, no one knew.

Shortly after the trooper arrived, the county officers pulled over. Things got kind of chaotic from then on, and the officers instructed me to step behind the yellow tape they had put up to secure the scene. I stepped back and sat down on the curb and stayed there until they took both the injured man and the man who was responsible for this tragedy away. The crowd had pretty much disappeared, with the exception of a few witnesses. The man behind the fence was her husband, and she was Kelly. His life was spared, and he recovered after many surgeries. The man who hit them is now serving twenty years in prison. He never did admit turning his back on Kelly; in fact, he denied it in court.

The day after the accident was a somber one. I had been pretty drained from all the emotions I had gone through. I had this unshakable urge to buy a charm bracelet; I had seen them before, and most of my friends had them. I was never interested until that day. I went to a store that I knew had carried them, and I bought one. It was a Nomination bracelet; to me, it was just a bracelet. I picked out a golden angel charm for Kelly and a red rose for my dad. Later that same day, I went out to my mom's house to see everyone. I sat out on the back porch with my grandma. We looked up at the corner as we discussed the tragic evening before, and we saw a few people up there. We looked at each other and decided to go to the corner and introduce ourselves. We knew that they had to be family because they were up there for quite a while, and it looked like they were trying to figure out what exactly had happened to their loved ones. We walked up and met Kelly's sister-in-law and her boyfriend. She wanted me to walk her through what had happened the night before, so I did. She said that it would mean so much if I went to see Kelly's husband, Darin, at the hospital as he had, understandably, been going through such a hard time. I don't know where the courage came from, but I went. I walked into that hospital room and introduced myself. Darin grabbed my hand and pulled me in for a hug. He had a hold on me that said everything: thank you.

About a month later, Darin called me and said that Kelly's parents were in town and wanted to meet me. I was chaperoning my sister's school trip to the air races at that time. I told Darin that I would absolutely be there and left immediately. My mind was racing the entire drive over to his house. What were these people going to be like? What were they going to ask me? I had no idea what I was in for, but I knew that I had to do it. When I walked into Darin's house, this woman grabbed me. She was sobbing uncontrollably. This had to be Kelly's mother. We sat and talked for hours. I told them that I would be more than willing to answer any questions they might have but that I wouldn't offer anything, as I didn't know what they were ready to hear.

That day, the day I met Kelly's parents, was one of the most humbling days of my life. It took me a long time to realize how these people, Kelly's family, could be so full of love and faith after experiencing the worst tragedy of their lives. They taught me that it was because of faith, that one simple word that we all know but don't always apply to our own lives. I am a better person today for knowing these amazing people; they have truly changed my life. As for Kelly, of course I wish we had known each other in this life, but she will always be a dear friend to me. The person I have always known but never met.

* * *

The gift she gave to Kelly. The gift she gave to us. Upon our return from Virginia City and Kelly's memorial, we stopped at that corner to place flowers for Kelly. I had bought two angels (from the Boyds Bear collection) to drop off for Denielle and her mom. I had also given them a picture of Kelly on her wedding day. I wanted them to have a different vision of Kelly. When they'll remember her, they will see her as she is in the picture, not that night on the pavement. Denielle was not there, but her mom was. We offered our thanks and spoke briefly and left. Darin rode home with us, and so did Kelly. We were taking her home. Over a hundred miles, I carried her with me on my lap. Childbirth is painful; a child's death is . . .

A light had gone out in all of us. Randy and I made a promise to Ted and Angel that we would survive this. They knew that this would kill us, and they had expressed that to us. I came to wish I hadn't made that promise. I wasn't so sure.

Ted lives over four hundred miles away. He was despondent and so full of hate and anger. I feared he would hurt himself or come after this faceless stranger. I am grateful Ted didn't live in Reno!

Angel was a zombie, in and out of a day that didn't belong to her anymore. She met Brianna and Ireland's needs, and Brian nurtured them. On one of our trips to Boise and after a day of concerns with what I was seeing in Ted and Angel, I felt so defeated. I wasn't talking to God at that time, so I had no one to help me with this. I couldn't fix this. I couldn't make it better. I wanted to disappear, to run from the pain of it all, never to return. This was not happening to us, to our family. We were touched by death. I wrote the following:

> *Oh, death, how you've deprived us and dared us to accept you*
> *You left us to walk your valley and forced us to climb heights in*
> *our weariness*

You came so unexpectedly, with no warning of your arrival
Can we not call on you when we are ready for and welcome you
You empty us and leave us void of life's sweetness
Do you sleep in your own darkness so as to be rested when we fight you
We do not fear you individually for ourselves
But the remnants of you for the loved ones who are left to suffer because of you
How we have tasted your bitterness and loathed your existence
You are not the end of us though—only an end before a beginning that you cannot revisit

Randy read the Bible, and I distanced myself from God's Word. I was afraid he wanted more from me than I was willing to give. I had read the New Testament a number of times over the years. I knew what he wanted. Instead, I reached for a little book given to me by a friend from Sacramento, a mother herself who had lost her son at the age of three. He got hit by a car in front of their house. This little book was *Bedside Blessings* by Charles R. Swindoll. I started reading. It was full of inspirational quotes and scriptures. I was reading the Bible! I was on my way back. That little book had some big words, words of comfort. I had bought this book for a few other people in their time of need. We went on to buy a few more books by Mr. Swindoll—*Simple Faith*, *The Mystery of God's Will*, *The Grace Awakening*, to name a few. A few other small books packed with some powerful words would be *Five Meaningful Minutes a Day*, *Perfect Trust*, and *When God Is Silent*. Thank you for your writings, Mr. Swindoll.

We had taught our children about the teachings of God. Ted was baptized on Mother's Day at the age of thirteen. He wanted to commit himself to the Lord. Kelly, in her innocence at five, cried openly when she learned of Jesus's death. Angel would pray individually for everyone (no wonder she went to bed so early). God, we thought you were pleased. We were trying to serve you, and yes, we fell short of your glory and were not without sin. We were trying to find our way back to God in our weariness.

By the way, Kelly was attending church in Reno and wanted to be baptized into Christ. She died before that happened. I believe she was baptized by her tears that day in our bathroom. Jesus saw that—the baptism of desire.

Months later, Ted was still blaming God. I was so scared for him. I talked to him one night on the phone about his relationship with God and how concerned I was for him. It would be months later before he shared something with me. He had gone out one day and bought himself a cross necklace.

I said, "I am so glad you did that for yourself."

He said, "I didn't do it for me. I did it for God."

In another call with Ted, we talked about how we couldn't handle the smallest things. His wife was four months pregnant and had had the threat of a miscarriage. Ted said, "If anything is wrong with this baby . . ." That was all he got out when his wife hollered. The baby moved for the first time. Our granddaughter was introducing herself and saying she was fine. I think that was a turning point for Ted.

There were so many wonderful people there those first days for us. Some family and friends remained constantly. My brother Larry would be one of those people. He is my only sibling that lives here in Susanville. He called often and would come and visit us regularly along with his son Jesse. We cried together. He sure loved our Kelly. They had this wonderful relationship. Larry would rib Kelly about something, and boy, could she give it back to him. He never learned; you didn't mess with Kelly. This was fun to watch.

I love my brother. Kelly had just recently shared with Angel, "You could sure tell how much Uncle Larry loved you by the way he hugged you."

We met Denielle on one of our trips to see Darin. By the way, Denielle and I share the same birthday. He called her (she was at the air races), and she arrived at his home in a few minutes. She walked in the door, and I threw myself into the arms of a stranger to me, not to Kelly. We spent three hours with this beautiful young girl who was the same age as Kelly. She majored in criminal justice, as did Kelly. She was caring and selfless, like Kelly. Randy would later share how interesting it is that you can spend your whole life with some people and not be close to them, and yet you can spend three hours with a total stranger and fall in love with her.

Denielle said she felt connected to Kelly that night and felt she always would be. She had been a strong source in our healing and in our lives. We continued to get cards from her and spoke quite frequently on the phone with her. We would meet for visits—she and her husband, Remo, at our home in Susanville, and we at theirs in Reno. Denielle was becoming a part of us. She herself was suffering from depression and the effects of all this. I encouraged her to back away from us. Maybe we were too much for her. "Protect yourself." She wasn't going anywhere!

That Christmas in 2003, Remo got very sick and fell in their bedroom. Denielle's grandma called 911. The ambulance attendant who administered help to Remo was none other than Matt, Melinda's husband. Matt, for a short time, had lived with Melinda and her roommates, Kelly and Shannon, in Reno. Matt knew Kelly very well but did not know Denielle and Remo. En route to the hospital, Denielle rode up front with Matt. Matt had seen the wedding picture of Kelly and Darin in their bedroom, and he asked Denielle, "Are you Denielle?" And she said yes. He knew of Denielle but had never met her.

Where Denielle and Remo were living at the time was not in Matt's route. He was covering for someone else. It was quite unnerving for him to see that picture in what he thought was a stranger's house. I might also add that Matt was the one who transported Kelly from the mortuary to the church for her memorial. His wife, Melinda, wrote Kelly's obituary. It would be a week or so after Kelly's passing that I would see Melinda during one of our visits at the hospital (with Darin), and she presented it to me. I said, "You wrote Kelly's obituary? How did you know I couldn't do this?" I had been trying for days. How do you do such a thing? I couldn't, and Melinda knew that of me. She had the obituary exact. She knew Kelly. She knew us.

My talks with Denielle became more in depth. I was learning more about her little life, and she with mine. There was a familiarity about her life. She too had been affected by and suffered loss due to drugs and alcohol. She had always felt very spiritual, but she herself had felt abandoned by God. The more we talked, the more she was renewing her relationship with God. We were helping each other. We grew to recognize that we needed each other. We both felt we didn't just happen; this was part of a plan.

Two years later, we were closer than ever. Like Angel had said, "I can't imagine us without Denielle."

Denielle works for Habitat for Humanity. She volunteers for a crisis center and is now working on another venture to help those who have suffered the loss of a loved one. She is also taking classes at University of Nevada, Reno. She plans on graduating in a year or two. With having to work, she can't go to school full-time, but she is getting the job done. If there were more hours in the day, Denielle will be filling it in some way as a service to others. Randy just recently had a serious talk with her about making time for herself. She said she was going to consider that talk.

Chapter Nine

Today You Became a Wife

I wish Kelly knew the influence she had had on so many people. We had heard so many praises, "I have always admired her," "She makes me want to be a better person," "I have changed my life because of her," etc. People did respect her and what she stood for. We all learned so much from her. An instructor she had at the junior college here (in Susanville), in a letter to us, stated that when Kelly spoke, it was like thunderclaps.

Kelly had worked at her job on her last day. She was asked to step in at the last minute on a court case for a fellow colleague. She performed her job in the presence of Senator Susan Leslie. Susan sent us a sympathy card and a letter expressing how impressed she was with how Kelly handled herself that day. That meant a lot to us. It would mean a lot to Kelly too.

One thing I do know of Kelly is that she wasn't boastful. She always tried to better herself. She wasn't that confident and sure of herself. She was so loving and caring and was affected by the hurts of the world. To us, there was such a grace about Kelly. Ted and Angel looked up to their little sister. They said she was older and wiser than them. She was like an old soul, as Angel had said. She was very loving and respectful of her mom and dad. She never gave us an ounce of grief. She loved hanging out with us—hunting, shopping, anything we had going on, she wanted to be a part of it. She was twenty-four years old—very mature, I might add—but she still called us Mommy and Daddy. We think that it was a term of endearment. God bless you, Kelly.

It didn't take us long to see what Kelly saw in Darin. We loved him from the get-go. After he lost his wife, he suffered with the fact that he hadn't protected her. Everything he did that night was all about protecting Kelly. He was a fireman, and he was in the business of saving lives. How hard this was for him. We mourned together, pulled together in our loss. He was so good at keeping Randy and me informed with the goings-on of the investigation and court stuff. Darin, of course, would be the first one informed of all things, him being the husband. He would be the one that would make all the decisions regarding his wife, but he would always ask what Randy and I wanted and would honor our wishes 100 percent.

He flew to Idaho on the day of Brianna's fifth birthday party to surprise her, something he knew Auntie Kelly would do. Many times he would pick me up from the airport and drive me all the way home to Susanville. He had never not been there for us. Every gesture was followed with "It is what I want to do. It's what Kelly would have wanted. She taught me so much." We couldn't believe what this young man, our son-in-law of nearly four months, was doing for us. It was almost unheard of. He was loving and honoring his wife. He was loving us. We are so proud of Darin and couldn't love him more.

Darin and his future brother-in-law, Joe, came this last summer and put in a pond and waterfall in our backyard in loving memory of Kelly. It is surrounded with all the angel statues and little creatures and plants that Kelly loved so much. We find so much peace there. Thank you, Darin. Thank you, Joe.

Kelly had a wonderful relationship with her sister-in-law, Robin. Robin and I had shared a wonderful talk about Kelly just a few months before August 13. I will forever be grateful for her kind words toward Kelly. They were the best of friends as well as sisters-in-law. I had a special card made for Kelly's wedding day that included a poem I had written for her:

Today

Today is a special day
Like all the days before
Today started for you some twenty-four years ago

You came a little early
You didn't want to be late
Today began for you in 1978

Today will be a memory
Like back when you were two
The memories you have of us
You know we have of you

Tomorrow you'll move forward
Yesterday is past
Live today in wonder
You're sure to make it last

So as you move beyond today
Into a married life
You can add to your memoir
That today you became a wife
I've loved you all your days
Mom

Kelly and Darin were married at the Venetian in Las Vegas on April 19, 2003, in a small affair (twenty people), with a beautiful ambiance. Kelly had picked the date April 19 to honor the grandpa and grandma that she loved so dearly. That was their wedding date. After we lost Grandpa Frank, Kelly requested to have a cross that grandpa had and had carried in his wallet during the war and ever since. Kelly wanted to carry this cross in her bouquet on her wedding day. Just as the ceremony was to begin, Kelly discovered she had left the cross in her hotel suite. These weddings were performed one right after the other, so you had to get started on time. Kelly was not getting married without Grandpa's cross. She requested a few extra minutes to have this cross retrieved. The minister obliged her. Her dad ran back to her room to get the cross, and she carried it with her bouquet. That cross sure stands out in her wedding pictures.

The wedding song was sung in Italian. Their reception was held at Zeffirino, a beautiful Italian restaurant. This was no dinner; this was an experience. It felt like we were in Italy.

I also have to let you know of the kindness we received from the photographers in their shop. After we lost our Kelly, there were a lot of requests for pictures and a few videotapes of her wedding. The sweet lady I had spoken with on the phone (this was in Las Vegas) had heard about Kelly and Darin. Her daughter was living and attending school in Reno at that time and she had called her mom to tell her about the accident. Her mom said she was crying. We got the pictures we had requested with no charge. They even made an enlargement later on for the sentencing. Again, no charge. Thank you, all.

Chapter Ten

Two Steps Forward

We were constantly moving two steps forward, three steps back. We struggled with just caring enough, enough to get us up in the morning. For months we didn't care at all. Now we need just enough to keep us moving. It was like on August 13, God said to us, "I'm going to have to take this life away from you. Here is a new one. Do the best you can with it." We are all doing the best that we can with it, but we want the old one back. Like Angel has said, "Okay, God, we have learned our lessons from this. Can we have her back now?" It hurt so bad because we loved so much, and God knew of our suffering.

I am confident in us. We aren't quitters. We have a tremendous amount of fight and a desire to honor Kelly and her life. We want her to be proud of how we have all pulled together through this. She would be devastated if this tore us apart. You'd have to know Kelly to know that her concerns would have been for us all. Kelly brought out the best in all of us. We miss not only the love we have for her but also the love she had for us. We know that God is in this, and he has his reasons and plans. We have to trust him; that's all we have to go on.

I love being a mom, the best job I've ever had. It's tough at times, even scary, but is so rewarding. I love children, the innocence of a child. God gives us this little life to love, nurture, and transcend into a thing of beauty—fragile, to be handled with care, with no instructions. He trusts us too. Things and money are not our legacy; our children are. The people we touch and who touch us are our marks in life. It says, "We were here." I heard this from an episode of *Touched by an Angel*.

My fears are for our other two children. They have a lot longer to live with this than Randy and me, God willing. I want their lives to be full. I want their hopes and dreams fulfilled. All suffering will end or, hopefully, be easier to live with. Life is not a forever thing. It is like we are all in school here, learning life lessons, with an occasional recess, waiting for the bell to ring when we all get to go home. From one end of the world to the other, we all started out at the same place, and we are all going to end up at the same place. God is just watching to see what we do in between, then he will decide the grade we get for the tests we have been given.

Randy burned all his time on the books at work. He returned to work in November. I was all alone now. How do I fill my days? Before, there weren't enough hours in the day. Now there were too many. I read a lot of inspirational books and watched more television than I had ever had before. I would go to sleep with the remote in my hand but would never shut it off. I quit watching programs I had once enjoyed. No news there was no good news. I could only watch comedy—reruns of *The Andy Griffith Show*, *Home Improvement*, etc. My all-time favorite program is *Little House on the Prairie*. I love the morals and values taught in this program. I found every rerun of these I could. I even owned some of the boxed sets, but I felt I was watching them alone. I didn't feel I was watching them alone on television; someone else was watching them too.

I have always been a dreamer. I would wake up the next morning and give you a detailed description of the dream I had the night before. For a year, I quit dreaming, except for five (I counted) dreams, mostly of Kelly—the good ones. I think Kelly did come to me in my dreams. I had woken up one morning at 3:00 a.m. and sat up straight in bed with the biggest smile on my face, proclaiming, "I am so happy right now." There was only one dream that could do that. After we lost Kelly, I didn't want to sleep. I didn't want to dream about her and the accident. I think I was protected from my dreams.

The forgetfulness was unreal. I was constantly asking my sister Peggy (she was here during our time of need), "Who gave us this?" "Where did that come from?" "Who said that?" My recall was awful! Randy suffered from this also but did better than me. We kept forgetting where we put this and what we did with that. I would find myself doing things and thinking, *I hope no one saw me do that!* One day, Randy even found money he had put aside and forgotten about. I would find a Mounds candy bar in my nightstand that I had forgotten I had put there. There was a lot of this going on. If it weren't so tragic, I told Randy then, that this was like Christmas twelve months out of the year. We kept finding these little presents everywhere.

I did talk to our doctor about this. He said that the first thing affected when you'd go through something like this would be your mind. He said that it would improve, and it had. I have been dreaming again, no bad ones.

We were all waiting for our healer—time. I couldn't wait for spring. I have always loved those new calves and colts I see on my way to town. Spring is a rebirth of all nature has to offer.

Spring came, and people were out and going for walks in their shorts and spring attire. Everyone was coming out of hibernation. They were out there living, and I envied them because we weren't. We needed time. Was it ever going to get here? It did.

It has been two years for us, and we are finding that joy again, the joy in our days so we can have the peace in our nights. I shut the television off now.

Chapter Eleven

Friendships

As time went on, which, I have to say, is fairly recently, I was seeing a lot of things presented to me. I had said after the loss of our daughter that my world was getting smaller, and I wanted to keep it that way. I didn't want to let anybody in. Well, over a short period of time, I kept thinking of this lady I hadn't seen in years. Her name was Enid. When I was a little girl, we lived next door to her. She was a really nice lady with one of the most beautiful flower gardens you could have ever seen. She would talk over the fence with us kids and our mom and dad. We kids would often play hide-and-seek over at her house because she had a lot of good hiding places and two cute sons. I found myself thinking of Enid all the time now. Man, why had Enid been so heavy on my mind?

I told myself that the next time I would go to town, I would go pay her a visit, something I had never done before. I had seen Enid many times over the years but hadn't gone to her home for a visit. You have probably figured out by now that we lived out of town because I always went to town. Well, the next time I went to town, I forgot to drop by and see Enid. I said, "Okay, the next time I go to town, I will go see her." She didn't leave my mind. I got up one morning and I was cleaning my kitchen, and there I was, thinking of Enid again. I dropped everything and headed to town. This was in March 2005. I stopped by Milwood Florist & Nursery to get her some flowers. I instead chose the Easter lily, all in bloom. I headed to her home. I pulled up front, and what I saw was a For Sale sign. I looked through the window, and everything was boxed up, the door was locked, and no one was home. I thought, *Oh, dear God, where is Enid? This isn't happening!* I went back to the florists (they also knew Enid and of my plans to go see her) and told them what I discovered and asked if I could use their phone. I had gotten the phone number of the realtor, and she was willing to share with me that Enid had recently been put in our local convalescent home. I had to go see Enid, but I didn't want to go there.

Twenty-some years ago, when my own grandma Jo was in there (the one who read us the Bible with the warm milk), Kelly and I had a bad experience. My grandma was an itty-bitty thing, not even five feet, and suffering from Alzheimer's. She didn't know me or remember me as her granddaughter. As I entered her room, I saw that she was slipping out of her wheelchair; the seat belt was under her armpits, and she was almost out of it. I was bending down and trying to lift her back up when she started swinging and cursing at me. I had never heard my grandma say a cussword before. I hollered for help, and a nurse came in to assist. I turned around and saw Kelly plastered against the wall with a look of fear I'd never forget. I picked her up and ran out of the room. I slipped on some urine in the hall, but I did not fall. I never went back there again, until Enid.

Enid had outlived all three of her sons (one in Vietnam, just recently her oldest son, one she had lost as a child of eighteen months from leukemia) and her husband. She did have a friend named Harry who went to see her daily. I learned everything about Enid from Harry. She had been put in the home in February, right about the time she was so heavy on my mind. I went in and saw Enid. She had suffered a couple of strokes and was crippled from Parkinson's. She could not speak clearly but was sharp as a tack. We would communicate by hand signals—one finger meant yes and two meant no. She had so much to say, but I couldn't understand her. I would leave so frustrated. After that first visit, I made a promise to myself that I would faithfully go visit her, and I kept it. She just loved to be rubbed down with lotion. Her little joints hurt so bad. It was such a simple thing that would bring her so much pleasure. I felt useful.

I had been seeing her for months when on August 29 (it was her birthday), I went to see her again. I knelt down to her as she lay in her bed. I was face-to-face with her when the attending nurse asked if I was family.

"No, she's just a friend from my childhood whom I came to visit to give a rubdown to."

As clear as clear could be, Enid spoke and said, "And I appreciate it."

I said, "I heard that." I looked at her. "Did you say you appreciate it?"

She said, "Yes." I started crying as I was giving her a kiss, and one of my tears fell on her cheek. With a tissue in her crippled little hand, she wiped away my tear and said clearly, "Don't cry."

I said, "I heard that too. Enid, today is your birthday, but you gave me the greatest gift." I haven't heard her speak clearly since.

I do get great anxiety at times when I walk in that home. What you witness in all these patients is a humbling experience. It is like they are all sitting and waiting. Me, I just want to check out and check in. I don't ever want to sit and wait.

I'm sure there is not one of us that hasn't said, at one time or another, "I don't ever want to end up there." Please don't get me wrong. I am grateful for the care that is given there. These places are needed. I wonder, why can't we be born old and grow young? We would have something to look forward to.

Enid is still with us. She is eighty-four.

I have started recognizing my own strengths and weaknesses at this juncture of my life, and I have noticed that I don't make commitments easily. I want to be a committed person in whatever I commit myself to do. I don't want to let others down, and I am not one who likes to have my days planned out for me. That probably came from years of being in a job where I never knew the shifts I'd work on or my days off. I couldn't plan anything. I like to keep my calendar open! I have soon discovered I'm committing myself to these things I've told you were presenting themselves to me. I have adopted the "I can fix this thing here and can solve this problem there" attitude. I'm trying to help any way I can. I feel that there are things in my life that aren't fixable, and I have grown so tired of feeling helpless. I am becoming useful in my days, and it's so satisfying.

Here is another one of those tender moments that I will keep with me forever. On a number of trips to see Enid, I would pass by an elderly lady named Annie who would always stop me and ask, "Am I where I'm supposed to be?"

I would answer with "You sure are."

She would say, "Thank you."

Every time I'd pass by her, we would have the same exchange of words. One day, I decided to stop and talk to her when she once again asked, "Am I where I'm supposed to be?"

I knelt down in front of her wheelchair. She backed up against the wall and said she didn't want to be in the way. It almost broke my heart. I told her she was not in the way.

She asked me where she was, and I told her where she was. "Well, it's kind of like a hotel."

She said, "A hotel? What am I doing in a hotel?"

I repeated, "It is like a hotel. You have your own room, and there are a lot of people taking care of you. For all the years you have taken care of your family, now these good people are taking care of you. Do you have children?"

She said, "Yes, I do."

I asked, "How many children do you have?"

She said, "Two or three, I can't remember."

I asked, "Are they sons or daughters?"

She said, "I don't know, it was such a long time ago." She then asked, "Is someone going to come and get me?"

I said, "They sure are."

She said, "Should I just wait right here?"

I said, "Yes."

She said, "I am so scared."

I told her, "You have nothing to be afraid of." I then asked her, "Do you know Jesus?"

She said, "Oh yes, I sure do."

I said, "And God."

She got choked up and said, "Yes, he has been so good to me!"

I then told her that God was holding her in the palm of his hand, so she had nothing to be afraid of. She simply said, "Okay."

She didn't remember how many children she had or if they were sons or daughters, but she sure remembered Jesus and God. An hour later, as I was leaving the home, I passed by her once again, and she said, "Excuse me, am I where I'm supposed to be?"

I said, "You sure are, sweetie."

Another gift that came to us was the gift of friendship. After the first of this last year (2004) and the winter blues had really set in, we would get a phone call from Randy's friends (and I might add, identical twins) Gene and Dean. They had something for us to consider and would be coming over in thirty minutes. We didn't know what they were up to.

First, I need to let you know that just a few days before, Randy and I were really feeling the walls closing in on us. I told Randy we couldn't sit around here and wait for things to happen for us. We needed to make them happen. To go find something we could do to fill our days. We used to go to Reno for entertainment (there was just not a lot of that in Susanville during the winter months), but we hated going there anymore, and when we did have to go, we couldn't wait to leave. It wasn't the same anymore. I told him we seemed to keep talking ourselves out of everything and finding excuses not to go anywhere. It was not a good day.

Gene and Dean showed up with an invitation to go on a cruise to Mexico with them and their wives, Mona and Mitzie. They had already gotten their tickets, and asked us if we would like to go. Five minutes later, we were on the phone, making reservations. We did hesitate a little because we realized it was the same cruise Kelly and Darin had taken on their honeymoon, and the cruise would be the week of what would have been their first anniversary. Gene and Dean did not know this. I excused myself and headed to the kitchen. I didn't want them to see me cry. They had seen enough of that. They were one of the first ones there for us that night. I looked out the window, talked to Kelly, and felt she would want us to go and see all that she had seen and have the same fun that she and Darin had shared together. She talked nonstop when she had gotten back from their Carnival Cruise about the fun trip they had together.

I went back in the room, and with Randy, who recognized what I recognized, we made the decision to go. When Randy and I married in 1970, Randy had just started a new job, so he was unable to get time off for honeymoon. We had said for years that we would take one someday, but we never did. We considered this the honeymoon we never had. I guess that at this age and time, when the honeymoon was over, at least we could say we got thirty-four good years.

We had never cruised before. This was going to be new! You see, if you give yourself enough time, you can talk yourself out of anything. We didn't give ourselves the time.

The cruise wouldn't be until April, but we had to go shopping and shopping some more. The next couple of months would be about getting ready for the cruise. We were filling our days. It finally came, and we were off to a fun-filled vacation. We had a good time. Sunbathing and food, shows and food, dancing and food. So much food, and it was all good. We did leave the ship for horseback riding (thanks, Mitzie) and kayaking, but we couldn't wait to get back to the ship. By the way, by the end of the cruise, it was common knowledge among our group that it was my ship. I loved my ship! As good as all the food was, my favorite part of our dinner was our servers. They were Monica from Romania and Katie (not her real name) from Ukraine. Now, Monica was most entertaining and always pulled stunts on us. From the first night, she seemed fond of Randy. He was addressed as Sir Randy, and I was Lady Jan. You talk about feeling like royalty.

Monica had this bubbly personality with a tremendous sense of humor. One night, she just didn't seem herself. I asked her if everything was okay. She said, "Oh, is it showing?"

I told her, "We've come to know you well, and we can tell something is wrong."

She confided in me that she and her fellow server had a riff. She said it was her fault. She said she was such a perfectionist and that she had overreacted. I told her that after dinner, I would need to talk to her.

She said, "Did I do something wrong?"

I told her, "You have done everything right."

After dinner, she came and got me for that talk. We sat down, and I shared with her what this cruise meant to us. I told her about Kelly and how our friends were helping us to live again and that her professionalism had contributed to it. After her condolences, she shared with me that she was homesick. We hugged and cried together. It was a very tender moment. She told me that she had bought a time-share at Lake Tahoe for the next winter and asked if I would come and see her. Lake Tahoe is just West of Reno in Sierra Nevada. She wanted me to go snow-skiing with her. I told her I hadn't skied in over thirty years, but I would come and see her and maybe we could share some hot chocolate around the fire. She said we could do the bunny slope.

AN EARLY LIGHT

The last night of the cruise, as Monica and I were saying our goodbyes, she said, "I make promises to no one, but I promise you, you will hear from me again." We exchanged phone numbers and addresses. She has been true to her promise; she has called me twice. We are still planning on seeing each other on the bunny slopes in Lake Tahoe in March. She is also planning on coming to Susanville to see all of us. I told her we would all get together and have dinner. I told her that this time, we'll serve her!

On our way to Reno and the airport to start this vacation, as you can imagine, we were all pretty excited. We visited each other and listened to music. I brought along some music I felt would set the mood for our trip. One song was called "The Coconut Song." We played it over and over. If you aren't familiar with this song, I can only tell you that it is an upbeat, fun little song and appropriate for the cruise. Well, we all decided to make this our theme song for our vacation. It was decided that every time someone would start talking shop (about work), we would burst out into singing this song. Almost every night over dinner, someone would make the mistake of talking shop, so we would sing. We were sure that the other guests in our dining station were wondering, *What is up with that song?* Monica did ask about this song and why we kept singing it. She seemed enthused about it. One gentleman did inquire about it and went on his computer and had the song printed out. He made a dozen or so copies and gave these to us.

As I was saying, Monica always had something up her sleeve for us. One night, she even had her fellow server convince us that she was sick and was dropped off at the last port. I was so upset, as I had become very fond of her. I said, "We have to turn the ship around. We have to go get Monica!" It was with that that the curtain by our table was thrown back, and in the window stood Monica. Well, that night we took that sheet music and passed them out to our fellow guests, telling them to sing along with us when we signaled them to. We located a CD player, and it being our last dinner in the cruise, we busted out that song. We got out of our seats and danced to "The Coconut Song" for Monica. Everyone sang along. I wound up giving that CD to Monica as a memory of the time we had shared together. The week went by so fast, but the fun of it lasted long after, the memories of it forever. We were living again! Thank you, Gene, Dean, Mona, and Mitzi. We weren't cruisers before, but we are now. We can't wait to plan the next one.

Chapter Twelve

Balloon Story

This was such a beautiful experience you would have had to have been there to appreciate it. One year later, on August 13, Angel suggested we release balloons in memory of Kelly. She went to Milwood Florist & Nursery and got the amount of balloons that would be needed. They were filled with helium, and one in particular lacked this gas, so they did not charge Angel for it. We all wrote messages on them for Kelly. The one that was chosen for Darin (he had to work that day, so he was unable to be there) was a heart-shaped one that bared the words *I love you* as his sentiment. This was that *one* balloon.

At six thirty that evening, there were the most beautiful rays from the west. So white and brilliant I took a picture. There had been the threat of a storm that day, but nothing developed of it. The sky was clear, except for some scattered clouds. At eight o'clock, we were about to release the balloons, but it didn't look like we were going to get the sunset we had hoped for—the sunset in memory of Kelly and the last thing she enjoyed with Darin that night. We released the balloons and just watched as they headed up to the heavens—all of them, except two, bunched together and headed straight up. Angel's went westerly up and over a mountaintop in the distance. Darin's, however, was slowly moving more northwest, away from all the others. We were all rooting it on to pick up elevation, and as this was taking place, a sunset was developing. The most beautiful, awesome sunset you could have ever seen, with those rays I was talking about earlier. Darin's balloon slowly headed right into the heart of that sunset. Remember, this was the balloon that was not expected to ascend. It was all so spiritual! I have pictures of the sequence of this. The beauty of it all was so peaceful.

Because of the beauty of this experience, when time came for a book title, I decided on *The Heart of a Sunset*. It was a done deal and needed no discussion. Until one day, I was sitting and thinking about Kelly and how she had been called home so soon. How she had seen "an early light." I decided to change the title to that (*An Early Light*). I called Shannon to ask her opinion. She approved and thought the title was fitting.

The next morning, I called Angel to chat, and she shared with me how tired she was because she had been startled awake in the middle of the night by a lamp that came on by itself. It was one of those touch lamps. Brian went to check on the kids and checked out the house. Angel had a hard time going back to sleep as she was trying to figure out what caused the lamp to turn on. Brian said, "It was Kelly, okay? Now go back to sleep!"

We talked a while, and then I shared with her about my changing the title of my book to *An Early Light*. She responded with "Mom, do you get it? That explains my lamp coming on. An early light." We both felt that was Kelly saying she approved too! Interesting?

Home

In the weeks and months following August 13, we were asked on a number of occasions if we were going to move to Idaho to be closer to Ted and Angel. We considered this, but this was home. The memories of Kelly and the memories we have of Ted and Angel are all around us here. Easter egg hunts out back, swims in the pond, and all our Christmases were spent here. We were whole here at one time, and we didn't want to leave that. The kids loved home. They enjoyed coming back to their childhood here. When Ted and Angel moved to Idaho, Kelly really missed them. She loved Reno and didn't want to be that far from Mom and Dad. We promised her we wouldn't move up there. We wouldn't leave her either. Besides, Ted and Angel really weren't that far away from her. The drive to Susanville takes ninety minutes, the flight to Boise one hour.

Susanville is a small town with beautiful mountains and lakes, good camping, hunting, and fishing. This little town offers a lot, if you are willing to search it out. We have the best of both worlds here. We have all that nature has to offer. If you want the city life and dinner shows, Reno is a short distance and a pleasant drive.

We made many trips to Reno over the years; it was always a big deal to the kids. All we had to say was "Anybody want to go to Reno for the day?" and the kids would be in the car. Kelly said that Reno was like a second home to her. She knew her way around but tried to avoid the freeway (I am sure it's the small-town girl in her).

Kelly worked, planned, and saved for two years for her move to the Biggest Little City. Before she started school at University of Nevada, Reno, in the fall of 1999, she looked for employment. She was hired as one of the first employees at a new restaurant called Ruby River. She loved her job, employers, and fellow workers. She had come to know the many wonderful people of Reno as their food server. It was a great job that worked around her school schedule as well as the schedule of the other employees.

It would be a year later before she would meet Darin. She fell for him right away. Everything was blossoming for Kelly. Darin had grown up in Reno. Kelly's and his likes and interests were the same. They both loved the outdoors and were very adventurous. They fell in love and married a couple of years later. They had such beautiful hopes and dreams for the future. They were really good together and good for each other.

AN EARLY LIGHT

Kelly was born and died prematurely. She was anxious to get here, but she wasn't anxious to leave. Kelly was very structured in her routines of the day. She was very grounded in her thinking and observations in the events around her. I have to tell you that Randy and I saw this early on in Kelly. When she was about eight months old, she was strolling across the carpet in her walker and flipped up the corner of a throw rug. She backed up and straightened the corner of that rug. Randy and I looked at each other, laughed, and said, "We are not going to have to worry about her. She is going to be disciplined and tidy." And she was.

Early on, while attending Lassen Community College, she considered majoring in medical imaging. This was a field she was interested in, until one night, when she watched a coverage of a murder case on the Nightly News. She followed this case closely and watched, as everyone else did, the injustice of the case. Kelly was really interested with news in general and was always interested in the events of the world. One day, she proclaimed that she was changing her major from medical imaging to criminal justice. She wanted to go all the way to the Supreme Court.

While attending UNR, Kelly would often do her studies at the Wilbur D. May Arboretum and Botanical Garden in the Rancho San Rafael Park. She thought this was such a beautiful park. She was living on Sierra Street at the time, so it was just a short walk away. After the sentencing, Clyde's father donated a *Picea pungens Glauca fastigiata* spruce, and it was planted in memory of Kelly in the Songbird Garden area at this park. There is a memory wall in the park office, and we had a plaque placed there for Kelly.

One of the hardest things for Randy and me to do now is to go to Reno. There is no place we can go that we don't share the memory of Kelly. It is so hard, but I know that in time, it will become easier. Reno has been good to us, and it was good to Kelly. She loved Reno. She loved the promise of you. She wanted to build her future and dreams within your city lights.

One of the most painful times for me would come about a year later (after our loss of Kelly), on a flight home from seeing Ted and Angel in Idaho. For a few days during my visit, I had held in what I was seeing in them. Ted and Angel weren't the only ones suffering. Brian's and Ted's wives were beside themselves as to what to do, so much to deal with and overcome for such a young marriage. Ted and his wife had just been married a little over a year. They were tested in every way possible. Angel and Brian's children suffered too, witnessing so much.

Angel wasn't there emotionally for them. She took care of their physical needs. Our grandchildren, Ireland (one) and Brianna (three), lost their auntie but, in a way, lost their mommy too. So much time and so little progress. It was so slow in coming. As a parent, you want to fix all your kids' hurts. This wasn't something you could put a Band-Aid on. As I was dropped off at the airport, we said our good-byes and I cried. I couldn't stop crying, and I had no one to talk to. I couldn't control myself, and I was feeling embarrassed during the flight, so I wrote this:

To Live Again

As we travel through these most difficult days, we search in ourselves and one another a way to travel down this road full of detours to find ourselves again.

To live through and with the pain that has befallen on us so we may confront and find comfort once again in spite of the pain.

Fear has become our enemy, and we must destroy the destroyer. To rise above the hate and anger that have invaded and tried to keep company with peace and joy. Faith, hope, and love remain as they should so the other unwelcome guests could not devour us. Our hearts cry, but God cups our tears and wipes away our sorrow with his mercy.

We are not who we once were, the persons before our souls cried out to the heavens, where our love resides in wait for us.

We know not of our destination, though predetermined by us, only not known of an end we had chosen.

Only he who is greater knows when we will be brought together and be whole once again. He is our rock, our fortress, and our strength. If we lean on him, he will show us how to live again.

I hate that I can't hide the tears on a flight, where those who do not know me or my life story sit and wonder. I have to get out of here before I drown the plane. I can't control my heart.

We all have a life story. We are all looking and hoping for a happy ending.

Here is a quote by Elbert Hubbard (*The Notebook of Elbert Hubbard*): "God will not look you over for medals, degrees, or diplomas, but for scars."

In another flight home from Boise (months later), I brought Brianna home with me. The plane was full, and I couldn't find two seats together. I had let Brianna sit on one side of the plane, and I on the other. We were across the aisle from each other. She sat with a young mother and her son, who shared treats and visited with each other. I was seated next to a couple. The gentleman was reading (studying) the book of Matthew, and his wife was reading a book that caught my eye too. The book was *Waiting for Morning* by Karen Kingsbury. On the front cover, it said, "A drunk driver, a deadly accident, and a dream destroyed." It sounded too familiar. I struck up a conversation with them and came to learn that he was a minister. He and his wife shared with me that they had lost a daughter (at, I believe, the age of nine) some years back, and I shared about our own loss. I was at an entirely different place on this flight home. I received a letter later on from them, and the gentleman stated that our being seated next to each other didn't just happen. I felt it too. His wife sent me a book that she had found comforting, *Roses in December* by Marilyn Willett Heavilin. I went on to buy *Waiting for Morning*.

So often we would hear these words, "I can't even imagine." No truer words were ever spoken. I used to say that myself of others who were grieving. Most recently would be the Rocha family. I said these words so many times as I watched the coverage of their beautiful daughter, Laci Peterson. Not only can you not imagine the pain of losing a child, but the way they lost her was so tragic.

At one time or another, because of the love and concern we have for our children, we have said to ourselves, "I don't know what I would do if ever I lost my child." You don't know—you can't even imagine! Whenever I would send out sympathy cards to grieving families, I would struggle with what to say. What words are there that can lessen the pain? There aren't any, but knowing others share in the suffering means a lot. Knowing people are praying for you, even when you can't, is comforting.

Since our own loss, there have been too many families in our small community who have suffered their own losses. You are affected when you don't know these families but are more so when you do. You feel so helpless because you know the pain they are going through. You know the road they have ahead of them. They just have to travel down it and look for the signs of hope and faith along the way. I never thought we would or could come out on the other side of suffering. You are so consumed with the loss and pain it almost swallows you up.

Today I feel more alive than I would have thought possible. Somewhere in the depths of our soul, there is a sleeping giant that when awoken is bigger than us, bigger than life, but not bigger than God. When you cry from your soul, you are truly communicating with God, and he hears.

You have often heard it said to not take anything for granted—don't! What I missed, aside from the obvious, was the peace, joy, and happiness I had had in my life. What I wouldn't do to have these pleasures back. We are all getting there.

Chapter Thirteen

Tidbits

We all have our own cross to bear and have to weather the storms of life. Sometimes it is hard to stay in the light when darkness surrounds you. Adversity builds character, and God tells us how he won't put more on us than we can handle.

From the time we are born, we are being transformed from experiences and influences in our lives. All the little bits and pieces of our lives make up who we are and who we will become. Here are some bits and pieces of my life.

I was born on March 15, 1952 (the Ides of March) in San Diego, California, at Mercy Mercy Hospital. I was number four of seven kids, right smack in the middle, and I was comfortable with that. I was a breech baby, and I have my own thoughts about that. I had no sense of direction then, and today, I still don't. I always get turned around.

My earliest childhood memory was when I was four years old. I was sitting out front of a JCPenny store in Susanville with my siblings, eating an ice-cream cone. Grandma Kay had come for a visit and was shopping for clothes with Mom for all the grandkids. We all loved Grandma Kay dearly. She had that unconditional love for you and was a positive force in my life. She lived to be ninety-two. She passed away in 1994, and all her grandchildren came together at our mother's home in Oregon for her memorial. The night of her memorial, while my sister Adrienne and I lay in bed, I felt this large pocket of cold air above my face. I told

Adrienne that God was right there in the room with us, that I could feel him. I reached up with both hands and felt the pocket of cold air, then poof, it was gone. Later on, when I shared this with my sister Peggy, she said, "Do you think maybe that was Grandma telling you good-bye?" I think she was right. I just hadn't felt the presence of someone who had crossed over before. Grandma knew how much I loved her, how much we all loved her. I am glad she was part of my first memory.

We lived on Gilman Street and, later, Spring Street. Our dad worked at a gas station, and on weekend evenings, he played piano at the TNA Lounge for extra money. Our dad was a great piano player. He played by ear, couldn't read a note. We always knew our dad loved us, and we loved him.

Our mom was an only child, and here she found herself with seven kids of her own. I think we were too much for her. Seven kids would be too much for most people. I believe she did want and love us though. It was just such a hardship. I am glad for my siblings. We are what we have in one another.

I could never sit still, so I usually wandered the neighborhood, looking for pop bottles (two cents apiece). I would turn in these pop bottles at Royale/Idaho Grocery (a mom-and-pop corner store) for penny candy. My little brother Larry, however, had no resources, and at the approximate age of four, he went to that corner store, got one of their little carts, and started filling it up with groceries. He simply just walked out the door and down the street where we lived. The owner, Ignacio Urrutia, called our dad and told him that Larry had done a little shopping and was heading home. He said he would square up with Dad later.

Mr. Urrutia and his beautiful wife, Marceline, who worked side by side for years, have both gone to be with the Lord. Three out of their four children worked for years with their mom and dad and had kept those doors open for business. That says a lot these days, with all the big-store competition. I frequent it. It is like going home again.

I spent a lot of my summer days down at the millpond, catching pollywogs or visiting an elderly lady down the alley by the name of Lucy. She crocheted, and I was fascinated with that and her.

We had a local florist just a few blocks from our home, and I would stop there daily on my way home from school to see a caged talking bird they had there. I loved listening to that bird. It had a pretty big vocabulary. That flower shop is still here today (Milwood Florist & Nursery), and I still frequent it as it is a great flower and gift shop. No bird though, but real nice people who run it.

The school (Lincoln) has been vacant for many years, but I just recently learned that they are going to remodel it and make it into apartments.

The family to the left of us had two daughters, Betty and Bonnie. The father was a very quiet man, but the mother was very loud and mean. The girls were always in trouble and getting hollered at. Their mother did not like us kids and was always mad when our apples fell in their yard.

One day, the mother was yelling at and chasing after Bonnie around the house (a very small house) with a broom. I was rooting Bonnie on. "Run, Bonnie, run!" The mother stopped, waved the broom at me, and told me I was next. I took my own advice—I ran. I was around eight years old.

I believe our mom and dad did the best they could for us, but they just weren't happy together. If one of us kids weren't fighting, they were. It wasn't a happy home. It was sad but good that they divorced. I was ten when they divorced, and I went to live with my mom and her boyfriend, Dave, along with my sisters Patty, Peggy, and Barbara.

We moved to Sacramento for a few months then on to Tucson, Arizona. Patty moved back with our dad before this move, and Adrienne later joined us. It wasn't long after this move that Dave started pulling stuff on us girls. We really had to kick it into gear to look after and protect one another. We had to stay one step ahead of him. We would never let just one of us be alone at home with him or sleep alone. It became a game of strategy, and we constantly worked out our next move.

This is where the obvious and tough questions arise. It was so confusing to me then, and all these years later, it still is. Where was our mother in this, and why weren't we protected from him? Were we that afraid of him that we wouldn't tell Mom, because of the repercussions of telling her? Did she know and have fears of her own? For me, I was sure she knew, so I didn't feel I could go to her. I learned later on that this was why Patty moved back to live with dad. For her, Dave's behavior started in Sacramento.

I don't remember exactly when Mom shared this piece of information with us girls, but I have never forgotten it. She told us one day that Dave had had a head injury at one time and that he had a metal plate in his head. I remember thinking, *He has a plate in his head!* Years later, I thought maybe that had something to do with his bad behavior.

In November 1963, our half-sister, Lea, was born. A few weeks later, President Kennedy was assassinated. It was announced over the intercom at school. Some people were crying, but some were rejoicing. I couldn't figure out why anyone would be happy about someone dying.

From Tucson we moved to the deserts of Sonoita, Arizona, a short distance away. We lived in what Mom later would call a sugar shack—no electricity, running water, or indoor plumbing. We were introduced to an outhouse, lanterns, and a washboard to do laundry with. We hauled water from a big water tank nearby and took our baths in a small blue plastic boat. We rode a school bus, where roadrunners raced us, to a one-room schoolhouse (grades one to six). The schoolhouse was across the road from what was known as the Thurber Ranch, where we would go on an occasion to do crafts. I learned how to do papier-mâché there. It was my understanding that Dorothy Thurber, at one time, was the schoolteacher at the one-room schoolhouse.

Dave worked in the mines there, and his payment usually was in the form of food. His boss would show up from Tucson every few weeks with boxes of groceries, where the Hillbilly Bread sat on top. Sometimes his boss would be days late with the payment, and we would go without. We really knew what it was like to go hungry. I really appreciate the experience of this.

One day at school, a girl shared her fried bean sandwich with me. I was so grateful to her. I didn't ask; she just offered it. To this day, every time I eat refried beans, I remember her gesture.

One day, we went to a small town called Greenville, Arizona, where they were having some kind of street activities. I loved watching the square dancers. They also had drawings (tickets), where you could win a bucket of dairy products. We wound up winning two buckets! We really hit the jackpot that day.

Another time, after Dave received payment in the way of money, he took us to Tucson to McDonald's and the drive-in movies. We went to see an Alfred Hitchcock movie, *The Birds*. It scared me so bad. I was now afraid of the birds as well as all the other desert creatures.

AN EARLY LIGHT

We moved from Sonoita to Phoenix, Arizona, in the middle of the night. We kids didn't even know we were moving. I had a great distance to walk to school, and I could get a ride to school by Dave if I did him a favor. I didn't care the sacrifice. I wasn't doing him a favor. The school was close to an airport, and I would watch the planes as they would descend. I would stand in awe at the size of the belly of one of those things.

One day, it was storming out, and Mom told Dave he would have to give me a ride to school. Our mother didn't drive. She had a fear of driving. School was one direction, and we headed another. He pulled off the road and parked. I didn't know where we were, but he wanted a favor. I pulled away, got out of the car, and started running. I was going to be late for school, really late! The rain did let up, thank God. I started heading in the direction of the airplanes. As soon as I saw their bellies, I knew I was almost there. Somehow, I wound up on the backside of the school, with a long chain-link fence and residential homes on each side. So close and yet so far away. I was very late, but I made it to school.

On my way home, I stopped an ice cream truck and bought myself a cup of orange sherbet and vanilla ice cream with a little wooden spoon. I was eating and heading home when I came to the realization that us girls were on our own in this. I didn't feel we had anyone we could share this with. I think that's when I developed the fire and fight in me. This was the early sixties, and we weren't encouraged to share such things with teachers, neighbors, etc. This was a family secret.

The first time I tried to share with Mom about Dave's shenanigans was after his passing several years ago. Before I could get out what I wanted to say, she said, "I wish to God you girls will let the man rest in peace." The other girls had shared or tried to share of this time too. I didn't share with her what I was trying to share with her that day until after we lost Kelly. I wanted to scream out what I had been holding in for years. I hadn't been able to live in peace with it.

From Phoenix we moved to the beautiful town of Telluride, Colorado. I don't think I had ever seen a more beautiful site than I did in those mountains surrounding that little town. The scenery was truly an awesome sight! After spending a winter in Telluride, our dad came to get us girls. Dave had gotten paid and skipped town for a spell, so Mom called Dad to come and get us. All this had to have been hard on our Mom. Under the circumstances, I am sure she did the best she could.

This wasn't an easy time for her either. On Dave's deathbed, he wrote a note to Mom, asking us girls to forgive him. I already had.

The choices and decisions I have made in my own life regarding the protection of our children from this man have cost me a relationship with my mom. I have come to understand better today the strengths and weaknesses in others as well as myself. It is not necessarily a choice but maybe a habit that may have been formed years before. I know that forgiveness comes in all forms.

Forgiveness is an interesting thing. How can you forgive this big thing over here and not this little thing over there? I believe it has to do with the transgression and whether it was intentional or not. I have to separate myself from that person, and then, over time, I can forgive. I'll know it when I do; I feel it. When we learn compassion, we learn forgiveness. There have been many things I have either thought, said, or done that I needed to be forgiven for. If I haven't yet, then I hope someday I will be. I know that God has; that is a given.

Here is one of those little things I had to forgive. Back in the early nineties, Randy bought two new sets of Christmas lights for our big blue spruces in front of the house. As these trees grew, we had to buy more lights. Each tree used about ten to fifteen strands, and they weren't easy to synchronize. These were the motion lights with about ten different motions. Our neighbors always commented on how much they enjoyed our trees. Randy had spent hours with a tall ladder, decorating them. The first night we lit them up that year, someone cut some of the light boxes off. Randy hasn't decorated them since. Why? Like Angel would say, "Let it go, Mom." I forgive you, you idiot. I have to every Christmas.

Soon after our return home from Telluride with Dad, he remarried. Our stepmother, Lloyd, had a son, named Larry, and a daughter, Sandy. All the males in our family were named Larry—our dad, brother, and stepbrother. At one time, there were nine kids under one roof, all close to the same age, in *puberty*. Boy, was that a fun household. I moved out my senior year, and Randy and I married the summer after my graduation.

I should add that Lloyd came to be very loving and supportive of us kids. She and Dad divorced some twenty years ago. We might not have been popular with each other while under one roof, but as we grew, so did our relationship. She had never not been there for us kids.

I can honestly say that I learned more and grew more because of this time. I took more away with me due to the experiences, and I feel that I have grown more because of it. I am glad for the trials. I am glad for the lessons.

These are just a few bits and pieces that have built, strengthened, and encouraged me to never give up. For sure, I have my days when my knees buckle under me and my insides are like mush, but I have this drive to never give up.

Chapter Fourteen

Poetry

I started writing poetry some years back as a hobby. My sister Patty actually got me started on it. I really enjoyed her poems (she even had one published) and had expressed how I wish I could do that. She encouraged me to try. I use poetry as a way of expressing myself to others. The first poem I wrote was this poem "I Think."

I Think

*I think—that's what I do,
It's usually about all of you.
Rarely a sentence I began,
Without these two words, you understand.
So I thought if you had the time,
You'd hear me think in a rhyme.*

When our kids were all grown up, they liked to tease me about how I used to wear out the carpet to their rooms when they were in trouble. I would come back in with "And one more thing." It was important to me that they knew what they were in trouble for and why I was so upset. I never wanted them to wonder, *What did I do wrong, and why is she so upset?* I wanted to talk about it! Years later, I would write this poem:

Words for a Child

If I told you that I love you
a couple times a day,
would you ever wonder
these words I did say?

I'll make the time to spend
with you in my busy day
because you're more important,
a message I want to convey.

I want you to be confident
in all you say and do.
I'll give you words of encouragement
and say, "I'm proud of you."

Please don't ever fear me.
I'm someone you can trust.
I'll be your protector,
fight dragons, if I must.

I'll build you up,
not tear you down.
Your self-esteem's at stake.
I'll want to do this early
or realize I'm too late.

I will not make you promises
I know that I can't keep.
But I will love you unconditionally,
awake or when you sleep.

Kelly had to give a speech in one of her classes. It was to be of a celebratory nature, memorized, and so much time in length. We thought it would be easier to memorize it if it were done in the form of a poem. This will always be one of my favorite poems because of the time we spent together on it.

JANICE TASSI

Anniversary Celebration

*Earl met Pearl, it was meant to be,
One summer's day, under an apple tree.
Six months later, they vowed to be
Husband and wife for eternity.
Farming was the life they knew;
They planted crops, and soon they grew.
Hard work is what they faced each day,
Saving but a little for a rainy day.
The year was 1931 when
Pearl gave birth to a son.
Baby John would be the mister,
But two years later came twin sisters.
Sarah and Grace would complete the family,
Except, unexpectedly, came baby Emily.
The years they flew, the children grew.
Joy and laughter was what they knew.
There would be picnics down by the creek,
Church on Sunday—the first day of the week.
There was a war Earl talked about,
One no one could figure out.
The war was tough on everyone;
The loss of life affected some.
Now all three girls, including John,
Would fall in love and marry young.
Now that's how I came to be;
My parents started a family.
For Earl and Pearl, there would always be
Another grandchild upon a knee.
Summer vacations were lots of fun,
Home-baked goodies and a tractor run.
And you could bet under the Christmas tree
Would be a sweater Pearl knitted till way past three.
Now Grandpa was the talker of the two;
He told of stories about me and you.
Grandma, she would tuck me in,
A pat on the head, and a kiss on the chin.*

AN EARLY LIGHT

As far back as we can remember,
The love we felt kept us warm in December.
Pearl and Earl are special, you see.
They mean everything to you and me.
So on this day let's celebrate the very day that they first met.

Brother Larry's Fiftieth Birthday

The golden years are closing in
Puffy eyes a sagging chin
Wrinkles start appearing
Where your dimples used to be
A plastic surgeon is the remedy
Crow's-feet are a sure sign
That the years are not a few
A local podiatrist cannot pull you through
When the hair on your head is thinning
But the rest of you is not
You can find a patch or two
In a conspicuous spot
You get the heebie-jeebies
Bowels don't move—clogged arteries
There is no tone
Just brittle bone
You suck it in—a double chin
A doctor's number on speed dial
Medic alert gives you a while
We have Depend underwear and Medicare
Rite Aid and Medicaid
They say that man is different
Than his counterpart
While she is aging gracefully
He's called an old fart
You are heading for retirement
In a year or two
Don't bank on Social Security
It's not there for you

JANICE TASSI

You know how much I love you
My little brother still
I'll love you now and always
Don't forget your little blue pill

Love,
Janice

Sister Patty's Sixtieth Birthday

How lucky are you, look where you have been
From Orange Crush and Kool-Aid to vodka and gin
Man on the moon, the Vietnam War
Route 66 in a classic old car
The Beatles and Beach Boys, Elvis and Stones
Songs on the radio to follow you home
Annette Funicello, Liz Taylor, and Wood
Ann-Margaret and Welch—boy, were they good
Redford, Paul Newman, Brando, and Dean
Hot young actors to light up the screen
Cassidy and Sundance, John Wayne, "the Duke"
Westerns or drama, Cool Hand Luke
Scenes from The Graduate *or* Bonnie and Clyde
Gidget or Psycho, *best friend by your side*
Romeo and Juliet, to sir with love
Romance at a drive-in, moon and stars above
Girls in miniskirts, guys a tie-dyed tee
Hippies at Woodstock, pot and LSD
Malt shops with colas, burgers, and fries
Songs on a jukebox playing 45s
How lucky are we, look where we have been
Chance or choice, we'd do it all again
Happy 60's birthday

AN EARLY LIGHT

Ted, Our Sports Fan

When you were a little man
You played with boxes, a pot, or a pan
You entertained yourself so well
A toy store-bought or a household pail
Wiffle ball, a neighborhood fort
Shooting hoops on the basketball court
Bicycle jumps in Verdun's backyard
Collecting a football or baseball card
Sports has always been your thing
You didn't go pro, no NFL ring
Competitive, you've always been
You hate to lose, strive to win
Admire your dedication to the Saints
If I recall, the fans call them Aints
The Cardinals, the Pistons
NASCAR for the Winston
A birdie, a bogey, or hole in one
Golf on a course close to home
Hunting and fishing with Dad and Ol' Blue
Watching Wimbledon, I don't have a clue
Just so you don't think I'm a joker
I believe the game now is poker

To my beautiful daughter Kelly Dawn, I love you more than words can say

(2006)
Fire and Ice

At the dawn of a new day
you announced your arrival
Like the snow of the season of
his birth, you gently came to us

So quiet and soft a spirit lay
nestled in a heart full of goodness

JANICE TASSI

*Generosity like a treasure found
at the end of a rainbow that would
yield lives enriched*

*Kindness that was practiced like
the orchestrated birds in spring*

*A smile that could touch and warm
an iceberg and light up the
ocean's floor*

*You stood tall in grace and beauty
as an unshaken redwood in
all her majesty*

*Such discipline as the hours on a clock
not off by a minute as to upset the rhythm and make a whole
world rock*

*A harvest of friends you have
as they gather in Thanksgiving
to have kept your company*

*The love—oh, the love—how strong
and yes, the greatest of the three
We are bound by love, not separated
but united in eternity
A life so accomplished as to
honor the artist who colored
the grand canyons and painted
a sunset just for you*

*Like an earthquake, tsunami
or a hurricane in tow
Your untimely passing delivered
up a gentle soul*

AN EARLY LIGHT

An eruption of pain and sorrow
flowed from within us—like burning
lava distances itself from the volcanic source
we ebb our way to the tides of soothing comfort

We are as the fires that bring forth
embers that will ash and
become part of the earth's soil

Our souls ride the winds
and reside in a mansion with many rooms

Chapter Fifteen

Memories

During one of our mother-daughter talks, I asked Kelly, "What is your favorite childhood memory?"

She said, "Going to the dump with Dad and Angel."

I said, "The dump?"

She said, "Yes."

Whenever she and Angel went to the dump with their dad, on the return trip home, he would turn from the highway to an adjoining highway and go one quarter of a mile to the Johnstonville store. Johnstonville is five miles south of Susanville. There, he would let them go in and buy what was once considered penny candy. I shared this with Randy and stated, "Did you know at the time you were building a favorite childhood memory?" Not Disneyland, not Great America, it was a trip to the dump. He went a few minutes out of his way and built a favorite memory. You think you have to do this great, big impressive thing? No, just a trip to the dump.

For Christmas last year, Kelly's friend Shannon made a memory book about Kelly for all of us. Early on, she inquired each of us to share our favorite memory of Kelly. How do you pick just one? She had also gotten stories from friends and other family members. I want to share some of those as they are so precious. Even though I had to choose just one for the memory book (it will be the first I share with you), here are a few others that are so sweet in spirit and nature.

A Scooter Christmas

Every Christmas season, Kelly would anxiously wait for the new Christmas catalog to arrive. She would circle all her favorite toys that she'd want to ask Santa or her mommy and daddy for. Well, one Christmas season, when Kelly was around ten years old, she saw a beautiful teal-green scooter in the Christmas catalog. She got out a marker and put a great, big circle around it. She really wanted that scooter, so she asked her mommy and daddy if she could have it for Christmas. Kelly's daddy piped up with "Oh, I can make you one!"

Kelly's daddy was always building something for one of his three children, but what he built didn't always work well. Kelly said to her mommy, "Oh, Mommy, please don't let Daddy make my scooter." Kelly's Daddy went to work right away to make sure Kelly got her scooter by Christmas. He used parts from an old red wagon and other worn-out toys. He began hammering away.

Kelly woke up Christmas morning and was filled with so much excitement she could hardly wait to see what Santa had brought for her. She jumped out of bed and ran into the living room. Well, sure enough, that Christmas morning, there was a scooter under the tree for Kelly. A homemade scooter, that was. Her daddy had built it with a lot of love.

Kelly, not wanting to hurt her daddy's feelings, accepted the scooter with much love and appreciation. Kelly went to her mommy and said, "I love the scooter Daddy made for me, but the wheels don't turn, and I can't steer it." Her mommy smiled and laughed and pointed to Kelly's daddy, who brought in the beautiful teal-green scooter with a brightly colored red bow placed on the handlebars. Her eyes lit up! It was a very merry Christmas!

Bad Treatment

When Kelly became a teenager, she had quite a growing spell. She had one knee that she kept dislocating. The doctor said that she was growing at such a fast rate that her knees weren't locked in yet. The few times that she did pop her knee out, it popped right back in.

One day at school, she had turned just right, and her knee popped out again. I had gotten up that morning and decided to do a deep-conditioning treatment on my hair. I put on half a tube of VO5 oil treatment. I was slicked up greasier than the Fonz. I got a phone call from a friend of Kelly's at school, telling me that Kelly had dislocated her knee again and that the school had called for an ambulance. This was during the time we had no jobs and our insurance had run out. I'm sure this was Kelly's concern too. Knowing that this had happened before and was not serious in nature, I told her friend that I would come and get her and take her to the hospital. I headed out the door, greased hair and all.

The ambulance had beaten me there, and the paramedics were with Kelly. Her knee was clearly dislocated. It was serious. It didn't pop back in on its own, like it had done before. I walked up to Kelly as she was lying there, and she looked at me and said, "Oh, Mom, I'm so sorry." She was referring to my hair.

I said "That's okay, honey" as a hall full of students and teachers stood by. The ambulance attendant asked if I wanted help putting her in my car. I said, "No, you take her and make her comfortable."

At the hospital, they called the orthopedic doctor, and he came and popped her knee back in. While at the hospital, I was to share our insurance information with them. I told the receptionist that we didn't have any and that we didn't have employment at the time. She asked if we wanted to sign up for Medicaid (ouch). I said, "No, we will accept responsibility of the debt."

Kelly's knee never popped out again after that day. She went on to climb mountains and even skydive. As for me, I have never done a VO5 treatment again. Not one person looked me in the eye that day!

A Blinding Drive

It would be two years before Randy got his academy date to become a correctional officer. The academy was in Galt, California, just outside of Sacramento. He would be gone for six weeks, but occasionally on weekends, he would get to leave the academy. He went and stayed at my sister Barbara's in the Sacramento area. Kelly and I would go spend these weekends with him. This was in February, so we still had to struggle with the elements of winter. On one of our return trips home, there was a light rain, causing some snow to run off onto a very muddy highway. After Truckee, California (thirty-five miles west of Reno), I ran out of windshield wiper fluid. We were on Interstate 80, heading east on a steep downgrade. Every car that passed us sprayed us with dirty muck. This was a Sunday night and after a weekend of skiers heading back to Reno. I couldn't see and could only travel a measly twenty miles per hour. I had no cleaner or towels to clean my window, so we got into Kelly's duffel bag and pulled out two of her T-shirts. They both had No Fear insignias on them. These were very popular shirts in the 1990s. We found humor in it. I had to keep pulling over to let the traffic go by and to clean my windshield again. When I had a good mile clearance between me and traffic, I would pull onto the highway again. Kelly literally would stick her head out the window to guide me down the grade—a little to the left, more to the right, and so on. I was so scared my mouth was dry, and Kelly was calm and encouraging. She could be so vulnerable at times and yet a rock at others. We must have pulled over a dozen times and continued this same routine until we got to Reno. I will never forget her strength that night.

Here are a few stories that have tugged at Randy's heart:

Sage Hen Hunt

From the time Kelly was a little girl, her dad would take her; her brother, Ted; and her sister, Angel out to the desert in Old Blue (the family truck) to see the wildlife. She loved being outdoors and enjoyed nature. Fishing, camping, and eventually, hunting were the things she most enjoyed.

When Kelly was ten years old, she was given the opportunity to go bird-hunting with her dad and uncle Ken, an opportunity that excited her to no end. So the night before Kelly, her dad, and her uncle Ken were to leave, Kelly was full of eager anticipation. She barely slept that night, knowing her dad would be waking her up any time to start the adventure.

On that chilly autumn day, Kelly was up before the sun, ready to go. They pulled up in Old Blue to one of the family's favorite hunting spots and began to assemble their shotguns and gear. Kelly was ready to make her dad proud, remembering all she had been taught.

Midway through their hike, half a dozen sage hens flew overhead, giving Uncle Ken the first shot. He took aim, shot, and missed. Upon missing, Kelly's dad said to Kelly, "He can't hit the broad side of a barn! If only I can get a shot like that." Well, a few minutes later, he got his chance. He shot and missed all the sage hens. Kelly said to her dad with a sly smile, "You shoot like Uncle Ken." A few minutes later, while Kelly was walking, she jumped at some sage hens right in front of her. Kelly calmly took aim and shot one time and got her bird. She then turned proudly to her dad and said, "Is that how you do it?"

Double Installation

After Kelly and Darin got settled in their new home, Darin came home one day to announce he had found some cabinets they could buy for the garage. These cabinets were either damaged or missized in their construction and were not going to be costly. Kelly was anxious for the storage of them but told Darin that her dad had been waiting for years to get cabinets for his own garage. She said she would not get any for themselves until Darin hooked her dad up with some too. Randy purchased some, and Kelly got to see them installed in both homes.

To Be Safe

On one occasion, Kelly was at some kind of outdoor life event and came across some gun safes on display. The owners were Ron and Toni of the Silverado Safe Company. Randy had been looking at safes for years, but this was not a priority. Kelly knew this and knew her dad wanted to protect his valuables. She talked to Ron and Toni in great length about these safes and got all the information on them. Kelly called me and asked if I would come to Reno and meet Ron and Toni and check out a safe for her dad. I did, and with the Christmas holiday season approaching, I purchased one.

Ron and Toni offered me a miniature safe/bank that I could put under the tree. I put the paperwork in it, and Randy was going to be able to choose his own design, color, etc. Randy loved that safe and the effort Kelly had put into it. I might add that Ron and Toni fell in love with Kelly, as well as she with them. They continued to spend time together after their first meeting. They were greatly affected by the loss of her.

I feel that I want to add here that we had all the comforts of a home and were not deprived of anything. We were just raising three children and meeting their needs, but there were some sacrifices along the way. Randy always made sure that his family's needs were met first. He was just a typical dad who dreamed of these things and knew that someday he would get them. There was no hurry for him.

Trick or Treat

Growing up next door to Grandma Dorothy and Grandpa Frank's had its perks. Kelly, Ted, and Angel had access to a pantry full of all kinds of goodies. One day, while Grandma was at work, Kelly went over to raid the pantry. Grandpa Frank was asleep in his recliner, so Kelly quietly snuck into the pantry.

While she was in the process of retrieving her goody, Grandma Dorothy came home. Kelly did not want to scare Grandma, so she stepped into the pantry and closed the door. Grandma had done some shopping and was putting the groceries away. When she opened the pantry door, there stood Kelly. Kelly raised her hand up and said, "Hi, Grandma." Grandma Dorothy let out a holler. Grandpa Frank woke up and wanted to know what all the commotion was about. Kelly stepped out of the pantry and explained that she just wanted a treat but didn't want to wake up Grandpa and didn't want to scare Grandma.

The three of them laughed at the incident. Kelly stayed and enjoyed her treats and a conversation with these two special people she loved very much.

The Prize

When Kelly was six years old, her cousin Danny moved in next door with Grandma Dorothy and Grandpa Frank. Danny enjoyed living at his grandparents'. He especially liked having his cousins to play with and, well, Grandpa Frank's cookin'. His grandpa could make one heck of a breakfast. Occasionally, Danny would have to fend for himself and settle for a bowl of cereal. Grandma Dorothy always made sure she got Danny's favorite cereal—anything with a prize in it! Kelly, learning of the special cereals with the hidden prize, would go over to Grandma's and sneak the prize out of the cereal boxes. Danny couldn't figure out who was getting to the toy prize first. He knew that it wasn't Grandma and Grandpa. His suspicion turned to the only other person who had an interest in those prizes.

Danny knew Kelly was the culprit, but he couldn't prove it. One day, he heard someone getting into the kitchen pantry. He jumped up and ran over to catch the culprit, but he wasn't quick enough. The pantry was empty. Then he caught something out of the corner of his eye. He went over to the window and looked outside. There was Kelly, running home as fast as her legs would carry her, with the toy prize in hand! Danny couldn't help but laugh out loud.

Danny didn't share his knowledge of this with Kelly until years later. Upon hearing the story for the first time, Kelly's mom began to save the prizes out of the cereal boxes for Danny. Even to this day, at the age of thirty-four, Danny still gets his prize!

Staying Grounded

Cousin Joni, who is the same age as Kelly, would usually come and spend a week during summer vacation. Joni lived in Sacramento, so the girls didn't get to see much of each other. They were both very creative and found lots of ways to entertain themselves.

During one of Joni's visits to Kelly's house, there was a huge lightning storm. Both girls were lying in bed, afraid they would be electrocuted because they both had braces on their teeth. Kelly's brother, Ted, heard the girls' concern over the lightning storm, so he came into the room to comfort them. He told Kelly and Joni they didn't have to be afraid. All they had to do was hold on to the elastic of their underwear. When they asked him how that was going to help, he said, "It's like rubber tires on a car. It will help keep you grounded." They both fell asleep holding onto the elastic of their underwear.

Way Past Bedtime

Brianna loved her aunt Kelly, never letting her out of her sight for too long. Kelly took a trip to see Brianna and Ireland over Fourth of July for Ireland's birthday party. Kelly was given the option of sleeping in her own bed, but Brianna wanted desperately for Aunt Kelly to sleep with her in her bed. Of course, Kelly said yes. Spending time with Brianna was always so fun. Well, Brianna talked and talked until way past bedtime, and Aunt Kelly got very little sleep that night. Brianna woke Kelly up early the next morning and said she was hungry. Kelly responded with "Don't wake me. Go wake your mom." After a few nights of this same routine, Brianna's mommy told Kelly she should sleep in her own bed and get some good sleep. Kelly quickly responded, "No way, I wouldn't miss this for the world!"

Wanna Bet?

When Kelly learned that her sister, Angel, was pregnant and that she would soon become an aunt for the second time, she was thrilled. She already adored her niece Brianna and couldn't wait to meet the new addition to their family. Kelly kept a calendar, marking down the days until the birth of Ireland Grace. Kelly was so proud to be an aunt; it was one of her favorite titles. When Angel's due date got closer, Kelly made the trip from Reno to Redding, hoping to be there for Ireland's birth.

One weekend, Kelly made the trip to Redding with husband-to-be in tow, known to the family as Proud Uncle Darin. When they arrived, Darin made a bet with Angel. He bet that Ireland would be born while they were there for the weekend.

Angel asked Darin, "How much do you want to bet?"

Darin replied, "One dollar."

To this, Angel replied, "One dollar, four whole quarters, a dolla'!"

It was a bet!

Well, the weekend passed, and Uncle Darin lost his bet with Angel. On July 2, Ireland Grace was introduced to the world. Aunt Kelly gladly made the trip to Redding once again to see and hold her special, new niece, knowing they would always have a special bond. And you know, Angel never collected on that dolla'!

My Sister

Her smile warmed my heart. She was my buddy. At UNR, three days a week, I anticipated our lunch dates in the quad. They were special moments when we got to talk uninterrupted. We sure did grow to hate those power bars Grandma would buy for us in bulk. Her sarcastic wit made me laugh. We'd drag ourselves out of bed for an early morning math class we both could have coasted through without much effort. This all based on point deductions from your grade for absences and an unspoken competition to finish with the higher grade. We finished first and second out of 160 students. Most of the happiness I have today, I owe to her. She was precious. In 1994, she let me borrow her *Forrest Gump* CD in return for borrowing the movie *She's Having a Baby*. I had copies made and gave them to her, which she promptly, without my knowledge, switched for the originals. For years we quietly switched them back and forth whenever possible, sometimes leaving notes for the perpetrator. Just before leaving for Boise, I went to make another switch when I noticed she had several CDs of mine that I had blamed friends of taking. She was crafty. I let her keep them. I treasure every moment we had together, even more so the last one.

On her first visit to San Diego to see me (while in the navy), I took her out to dinner for her birthday. This then became an annual event.

I am proud of what she had accomplished and even more for who she was. I admire her choices in life and her unselfish character. She was our waitress at Ruby River for the first big date I took my wife on. Fantassi Jr., a.k.a. Kelly, was a nickname she was proud of and one she wore well. The two of us were so much alike in many ways. I would usually describe her as just like me but better, without the bad. For her I would plant pumpkins each year for the kids, nieces, and grandkids, as our grandfather had done for her each year, one of my fondest memories. Kelly Dawn, my inspiration, my friend, my little sister.

In my heart always,
Ted

Are You Sleeping?

Kelly and her friend Melinda were invited to go on a trip to beautiful, sunny San Diego. They were thrilled for the opportunity to go lie on the beach, explore the town, and create new memories.

When they arrived at the hotel suite where they would spend the next week, everyone buddied up for a room. Of course, Kelly and Melinda gladly took one of the guest rooms, deciding it was much better than the fold-out couch!

Each day was filled with sightseeing, shopping, and beaches. Each evening, the girls would come back to the hotel, buzzing about the day's activities and dreaming of the next day and what adventures it would bring. Kelly and Melinda would go to their room at night, tired and glad to be getting some sleep.

One morning, while each girl thought the other girl was asleep, there was a noise outside the room. It sounded like a woman knocking loudly at the door and calling to whomever was inside. This happened over and over with no response from the hotel guests.

Finally, the noise was too much for Kelly, and she shouted in response to the woman's voice, "Yes, we're sleeping!" Upon hearing Kelly shout, Melinda couldn't help but explode with laughter. It was then that Kelly realized that Melinda had been awake and had heard the woman's voice too. Melinda's laughter was contagious, and it didn't take long for Kelly to start laughing right alongside her, although she didn't know what struck Melinda as so funny.

As Melinda gained her composure, still giggling and trying to speak, she asked Kelly what the lady outside was saying. Kelly responded with all seriousness, "She kept pounding on the door and asked if we were sleeping." Starting to giggle uncontrollably once again, Melinda explained, "No, Kel, she wasn't asking if we were sleeping. She was saying, 'Housekeeping'!"

Upon hearing these words, Kelly couldn't hold back. They both lay in bed laughing until their sides ached. Since that day, whenever Melinda hears a maid say "housekeeping," all she can do is smile and remember that summer trip and all the fond memories with Kelly.

"Yes, we're sleeping."

Melinda

Chapter Sixteen

Off the Richter Scale

Saturday morning, October 1, 2005, I woke up early, like I had the last few weeks since starting this. I had no more thoughts and no more stories to share, or so I thought. I was to wake Randy at eleven forty-five to get him ready to go to work on a double shift. After I got him up, I told him I was so sleepy and was going to close my eyes for twenty minutes while he showered.

I woke up at one fifteen and discovered Randy was gone. I was lying there, thinking how he had to put his lunch together and I didn't tell him good-bye, when I felt what I thought was an earthquake. I looked at the clock so as to document the time of the earthquake. It was one nineteen. Just moments later, I heard this voice I was familiar with. The words were a series of vibrations, my mind was registering heart rhythms, and the message was "You don't have to call me, Mom. I'm okay." I responded with "Angel." Then a voice, the same as Angel's, said, "That wasn't me." This was clear and not a vibration. I then knew it had to be Kelly—she called me Mom. I lay there for the longest time. It was like everything stood still for me. I tried to take it all in. I first had to call Angel in Boise to make sure she was all right, to make sure someone wasn't trying to warn me about something pertaining to her.

The words were spoken slow and drawn out. What did this message mean? I was shaking and had the chills. The experience was not scary but awesome. Angel was on the Internet with dial-up at the time, so I couldn't get through to her. I really needed to talk to her, to make sure she was all right. I finally got through to her, and all was well. She told me how she had heard that your loved ones can come through for you and it is in the form of a vibration. I had heard of this too but couldn't believe it was happening to me. After our talk, I calmed down and enjoyed the excitement of it. Now, I had to figure out the message. Why was that Kelly's message to me? Of all the messages, why that one? It would be after a few hours, but I did figure it out.

We got the Reno television stations here in Susanville, and there would be times I would hear of an accident on the route that Kelly took to work. I would call her at work to make sure she had made it okay. I also would do this when I would hear of an accident during the five-o'clock rush hour. I had to make sure she made it home safely. She was always to call us when she got home to Reno from Susanville. She was telling me I don't have to call her—she was okay! She made it safely to heaven.

Just the night before, I had written how I thank God for relaying all our messages to Kelly. I think he was allowing Kelly to relay a message to all of us. I did tend to worry more about Kelly, and I think that came from the experience I'd had back in 1986, after writing on the back of that picture. I was always afraid that there might have been some validity to it. God bless you, Kelly. Mommy loves you.

Here's another development that is pretty amazing, considering the timing of it and the outcome. Last summer, I was in Boise, waiting for the birth of our grandson Liam Kelly. I got this phone call from Randy telling me that I needed to call this lady who had some information for me about a sister we had always known we had but had never met. He proceeded with how he got this phone call from this lady (we have both known her for years), saying she was doing a family tree and was inquiring about my uncle who lived in Kansas. She said that she was related to my uncle.

Randy and she were sharing about the family tree, and Randy made this statement to her, "Jan has a sister who lives in Westwood that she knows of but not about." This is just twenty-three miles west of Susanville.

The lady said, "Yes, I know, and I know who she is."

Randy told her that she needed to talk to me because I'd always wondered about her. Some of my other siblings and I would often sit around and wonder. Sue (she has a name to use now) was another family secret. We didn't ever question so as not to upset those involved. Our father is her father too! She was born before our dad met and married Lloyd. Lloyd did know of her. Our dad never spoke about this daughter, and we felt it best not to confront him about her. Patty (my sister) learned of this sister years ago, and we had always kept the knowledge of her to ourselves.

I called this lady from Boise, and she had the first name of my sister for me, but she had married, and the lady was going to have to do some investigating to find out her married name. I had mixed emotions about where this would go and how it would turn out. I didn't want to upset anything or anybody. Maybe Sue didn't know about us seven other siblings. Maybe I should leave well enough alone. How would Dad feel about this search into his past that he had chosen to keep to himself? I needed to talk to my dad. I wanted his approval.

He said, "Her name is Susie," and he shared with me how she came to be and why he didn't have a relationship with her. It wasn't for me to question. These were his choices and decisions. I was happy to learn that he had kept a distant eye on her over the years.

I proceeded to move forward in my search. Before my life had changed so drastically, I probably would not have rocked that boat. These stories don't always have a good outcome. Why now? Why, in that time in my life, was that presented to me? I had a huge what-if hanging over me. I was willing to rock that boat, even if it meant I'd get a little wet.

This lady learned her married name and said she lived in Klamath Falls, Oregon (three hours north of Susanville). She said, "Do you want me to put the word out that you know of her and would like to talk to her?"

I said, "Yes."

The next night, I got a phone call. I was prepared for the rejection and the "Thanks, but no thanks," but what I got was just the opposite. Sue was overwhelmed and even maybe a little scared. She has two half brothers on her mother's side. She lost her mom when she was twenty. Sue had knowledge of her father and of her half-sisters and half-brother Larry. The door was open. We may not have had a past together, but we do have a future. Over the next couple of months, we corresponded by mail, sharing and learning about each other. I was able to answer questions about the medical issues on her dad's side of the family, sharing little by little what I called tidbits about our father and other siblings.

In our first conversation, Sue told me that she and I worked together in 1987 at the Susanville Safeway. I had worked there after the supermarket I was working for closed its union doors and reopened nonunion. Safeway was good enough to hire me and was graceful toward me when I returned later to a family of friends I had worked with for a number of years. Anyway, the year that Sue and I worked together, she knew I was her sister. I couldn't believe she had kept that to herself. She didn't know if I knew about her, so she kept silent. Sue worked in the meat department as wrapper, and I as checker, so we didn't work directly with each other.

It would be Christmas before Randy and I would meet her as a sister. What a wonderful meeting. Her brother, Larry, came over to meet her. How sweet it was. Larry showed up the next day with a dozen red roses and a gift for his sister. Next weekend was Easter, and Larry, his son Jesse, and I went to Klamath Falls to see her. Just a few weeks ago, she came to Susanville, and we headed to Reno to meet and spend time with sisters Adrienne, Peggy, and Patty. We had such a wonderful time together. Her sisters fell in love with her too. She just fit; it was like she belonged.

We were all so happy how this had evolved, and no one got wet!

That spring, I hoped that Sue would get to meet her father. He lived in Arizona. She said she would welcome the opportunity for that meeting. I got permission from Sue to share this story. She is happy to be a part of this book.

PS: Sue and Dad met in July 2006. It was a sweet reunion!

Chapter Seventeen

Today

Brianna was the only grandchild/niece who had known and would remember her Auntie Kelly. Kelly adored her little niece, and Brianna her. Brianna was three and a half years old when she lost her auntie. Ireland was one. These two little ones made Kelly anxious to have children of her own. Brianna had to witness so much sorrow and had experienced her own sadness in knowing they wouldn't be picking Auntie Kelly up from the airport anymore. You do everything you can to protect the innocent, but when you are under the same roof, it is hard to hide so many different, painful emotions.

It was probably a week or so after August 13 that I tucked Brianna in bed, and as usual, she wanted a bedtime story. She wanted one about Kelly. I told her a story and kissed her good-night. She always slept with the radio on, so I adjusted the volume. I was getting ready to leave when the song "Here without You" by 3 Doors Down came on. This song was very popular and really pulled at our hearts. Brianna said, "There is Kelly's song, Grandma." I nodded and turned away from her so she wouldn't see my tears.

I tried so hard to hold it in, but I couldn't, and Brianna said, "Are you crying, Grandma?"

I said, "I'll be okay, honey."

She peeked her head around and discovered my tears. She said, "Oh my goodness, I better go get my mom."

I simply said, "Just hold grandma."

She did, all three and a half years of her, not bigger than a peanut but so precious as she wrapped her arms around me, and she even patted my back as she did so. She was six feet tall to me. Grandma will remember this always, Brianna.

She is coming for a two-week visit along with her sister, baby brother, and her mommy. Her daddy will join them later. She has us lined up with all that we will do when she gets here. Brianna is a very happy, healthy six-year-old today. She is a kindergartner, has a lot of little friends, and is packed full of energy and joy. I better get rested up. Our grandbabies are a good dose of happiness.

Today, we are who we are. We will never be who we once were. We haven't overcome all things, but we have overcome some of the destructive ones.

Angel is doing fine. She has such a strong will and a tremendous faith. She has always been very confident and has never had self-esteem issues. That has weakened in her today—very independent in the past but has become very dependent. It is hard to stand alone in something like this.

Angel has always had such a bubbly personality, and she now strives to find humor in things today. She recognizes her weaknesses and is trying to build from them. I remember sometime back that she had told me that she couldn't handle the hate anymore towards Clyde. She prayed that God would take this away from her. He did that very night. She had been the first one of us to speak of one day forgiving Clyde.

Angel's husband, Brian, has been very supportive of her. He loved Kelly so much, and he himself has been greatly affected by the loss of his sister-in-law. He just recently had a Celtic cross tattooed on his shoulder with Kelly's initials under it.

Their home has so many pictures of Kelly on the walls that Angel says she's sure that people think she lives there. This comforts them.

Angel and Brian are blessed with three beautiful children, Brianna Angeline, Ireland Grace, and Liam Kelly. They pretty much work side by side in the raising of their children. They are best friends, and most of their time is spent together.

Angel and I talk daily. We have to touch base, more for security reasons than anything. We need the assurance that everyone is okay.

She is my link to how Ted and his family are doing. Because of Ted's and his wife's work schedules, I am never sure of when they are sleeping. I do hear from Ted quite often, but daily will not be too much. Like I have said, I need that assurance. Angel and Brian had only lived in Meridian three months before this devastating news. They barely knew their neighbors and had not made any friends yet. Today, they have the best of friends in their next-door neighbors. What a blessing!

Angel and I are closer than ever. We are strong for each other and stronger because of each other. We draw our strengths from each other. My daughter, my friend.

Ted is a big man of thirty-three years. He is still my little boy. The loss of his sister had reduced him into a fetal position. He was more despondent and withdrawn than the rest of us. It was like we couldn't talk about "it" with him. We could barely talk about Kelly. He could not have pictures of Kelly out. It was too painful. He was consumed by so much hate, anger, and rage. I was always so concerned with what he would do with it. He has stayed in it for so long he is just now seeing his way through and out of it.

His faith is shaky, and he has turned more away from God than toward him. When Ted lost his Grandpa Frank in 2000, he lost his best friend. Ted knew every detail of his grandpa's life. He sat through countless stories and never forgot one. He knew the name of every family member (we still don't) and friends his grandpa had ever had. Grandpa lived right next door, remember, so Ted, as well as Kelly and Angel, saw him almost daily. This man was so loving and funny. He was always in rare form. Ted had just become accepting of his grandpa's passing when he lost his sister. It was a long road back.

Ted has a loving and supportive wife, when he lets her be. His daughter is his joy and laughter. He really dotes on her. She is the best medicine.

Ted does now have pictures of Kelly out. He talks about her all the time. They were a lot alike in some ways—a lot of common interests and hobbies. They could really talk shop!

Ted and I have good conversations, sometimes hollering matches, but we usually end it with "Now that was a good talk. I love you. Talk to you in a few days." We don't always see eye to eye, but we have respect for each other.

AN EARLY LIGHT

For years I had pondered over the quote Ted chose for the high school annual his senior year. I don't remember if we ever talked about it or if it was his quote or if he possibly heard or read it somewhere, but I've never forgotten how deep it was. The quote is this:

We are afraid of life, afraid of death, and afraid of each other.

I have to admit I was somewhat troubled by the sadness and darkness of his statement. God never promised us a rose garden, but I would have liked to have thought he would have had a happier and more cheerful outlook on life. I've come to understand how much truth there is to that quote.

Once upon a time, there was a welcoming world out there, beckoning to be discovered and conquered by a just-recent graduate. The anticipation and excitement of meeting the challenges of life has got to be hard to maintain today. There are a lot more obstacles to get around today. The balance of life has been upset. Peer pressure is so much greater, with the need and desire to fit in at any cost.

Thin is in, and high is cool. Kids are taking guns to school. HIV, the war in Iraq, the premise of another terrorist attack.

The promised future and the mystery of it have been diminished. Our youth needs its hope back and a future like the generations before them had experienced. That's life today!

Death probably ranks the number one fear. For me, it's the when and the how. I trust in God and his promise that the end here is the beginning of an eternity. We can't take God out of anything. He is the hope and promise.

When did we become afraid of each other? We can still tuck our kids in at night, wish them sweet dreams, and promise them the bogeyman won't slip in, in the middle of the night and abduct them. We guarantee they will make it to the bus stop in the morning and cross our fingers they will arrive home safely. No one will ever think of luring a child out of a mall or communicate words of enticement on the computer. Who will dare rob a child of his innocence and his life?

Sniper shootings are random. We aren't the target, so what are the odds we'll take a bullet? Kids are throwing rocks over an overpass for the sheer entertainment. They really don't mean to take a life—it's just so much fun!

Look at the security we have today at our airports and borders. We are safe, aren't we? It will be almost impossible for someone to steal our identity and rob sweet Grandma of her little savings. All the bad guys are locked up, aren't they? With all the overcrowding in our prisons today, surely we have gotten them all! No judge will ever release a child molester or pedophile. Our children are safe, aren't they?

Will we overcome the prejudices like those spoken of in history books, or are we all slaves to the prejudices of the past, present, and future?

The skies are still friendly. Our high-rises aren't built on sinking sand. Nothing can bring them down. We don't have to be afraid of each other. Not much.

PS: I did find out from Ted that this was a quote he had read.

I am really amazed at Randy's comeback. He was so broken and fragile I was almost afraid to touch him. Little words were spoken between us those weeks and months after. We would just look at each other. We knew what the other one felt. We knew where our thoughts were and who they were of. We were so lost and did not know how to bring ourselves out of the pain. Randy is a pretty quiet guy anyway, but the quiet was too loud at times.

He lost his little girl, his hunting partner, his little Kel. I know he was talking a lot at work. Good talks with the right people. He was becoming faithful and hopeful. He was reading the Bible and the inspirational books I was reading. Randy did not like to read. He would sit in silence and read. We would sit, watch television, and hold hands. Very few words were spoken. He knew he would see his little girl again someday.

He has his sense of humor back. He can keep you in stitches at times, and he does it with a straight face.

A couple of weeks ago, we sat around, talking with my stepmother, Lloyd, who had come to spend a week with us. The phone rang, and Lloyd and I heard Randy say, "No, she is not here. She left me three days ago—oh no, that's okay, I have replaced her already. Good-bye."

He was talking with a phone solicitor who had asked to speak with me. He was heard another time saying, "You know what? When we bought our home, it came with windows. You are not going to believe this, but it came with siding too." This was like the twentieth caller on this same issue about windows and siding. We can all take lessons from this guy. They just won't take no for an answer. You can't say yes to all of them.

Recently, Katrina happened. It happened to all of us. We made our donation. There was also another concern at the time that needed help. Anyway, I got this phone call one evening, and it was an organization we had contributed to in the past. The man asked for a contribution, and I told him we couldn't afford it at this time. After more persuasion on his part and I again told him "We just can't handle it now," he said, "Don't you care that people are dying?" I hung up the phone, but those words hung on for a long time.

So often I look at Kelly's pictures and proclaim to her that this isn't real. This must be someone else's life. It doesn't feel like mine. In a way, it isn't. It doesn't belong to me anymore. I guess I just haven't owned it yet.

I ask God to bless Kelly for us and to embrace her with our love. I know through him all our messages are received.

I am grateful for the gifts he has given us in the midst of our trials.

I am grateful he has been there in this.

I am grateful for the hope of things to come.

I am grateful that Kelly was spared from the suffering of the loss of one of us. That's one thing she was spared from.

Kelly had a Siberian husky (Lakota Sioux) she got as a pup ten years ago. When she left for college, she had to leave Lakota with us. We loved her doggie too! A few months ago, Lakota became sick with diabetes. She had become blind, had lost a lot of weight suddenly, and was not getting her winter coat in. With treatments, we could buy her maybe six months. We agreed on the treatments. We didn't want to let her go. This had been weighing heavily on my mind since making that decision. We were just getting ready to start the treatments when on the morning of November 18 (Kelly's birthday), I found myself calling the veterinarian's office to say that we would have a long cold winter ahead of us and felt that Lakota would suffer through it. We were projecting to lose her come spring, the time of rebirth. We were considering putting her down, and via the receptionist, the vet agreed and asked when we would want to do this. I said, "Today." I wanted to give Kelly her Lakota for her birthday. This was very painful as we had to let go of another part of Kelly.

It was two days later that Darin became engaged. When he called to tell me, he said it was one of the hardest things he'd ever had to do. I cried like a baby. I apologized to him for crying and congratulated him. Letting go is so hard. I am not that strong.

Darin and his fiancée, Michelle, are planning a summer wedding. He has our prayers for a beautiful future. Darin deserves all the best, and we are happy he is moving forward. He recently made captain at the Storey County Fire Department, at the age of twenty-six. Life goes on even when it changes. It's supposed to.

Ironically, Darin and Michelle's wedding will take place on the same day as a scheduled dedication planned for Kelly. When Darin first told me of the planned wedding date (this was also the date of Darin's parents' wedding), I chose not to inform him that that was the date of the RMEF dinner and dedication. I felt he might change the date, and I knew that their wedding preparations had already been made.

I did just recently share the knowledge of the date with him. I hope he knows our blessings will be with him on that day. For Darin, it's like the end and the beginning are both on the same day. If you connect the dots, he has come full circle.

RMEF (Rocky Mountain Elk's Foundation) is an organization that Kelly had attended with her dad for years. She grew up with a family of hunters, and she herself loved the sport. RMEF dedicates time and money to managing wildlife. This event takes place once a year and is a fun-filled evening of good food, a most entertaining auctioneer, a whole lot of sporting goods equipment, guns, wildlife prints, etc., as well as friends. Kelly had won a few rifles herself (they also offer raffle tickets) while attending with her dad. This year, we have bought a rifle and will be donating it to RMEF in memory of Kelly and her love of the sport. We have had a plaque made and a special sling for the rifle. This rifle will be an auction item, and we look forward to a very exciting, beautiful, and yes, emotional dedication.

Just this past summer 2005, my three sisters Adrienne, Barbara, and Peggy (who lived with me in Sonoita, Arizona, with my mom and Dave) and I decided to make a trip back to the desert where we learned so much about ourselves through our trials. It has been forty years now. A few people would ask us why we would want to ever go back there. For me, I wanted to go back to the place I had first accepted God into my life. I wanted to see that cross on the mountain that reminded us that we weren't alone. I wanted to stomp on that ground and say, "You didn't beat me." I knew this was how my sisters felt as well. This was to be a spiritual journey for us.

This time I'm speaking of, when I first accepted God in my life (age twelve), would be after a very frightening experience I had with my sister Adrienne. The four of us girls shared a bed (two at the top and two at the bottom.) One night, before I went to sleep, I saw a scorpion on Adrienne's shoulder. She was lying at my feet, sound asleep. With no room for error, I flicked it off her. I lay back down and cried as I was so scared. I looked out the window toward heaven and said, "I don't know who you are, but I know you are out there," and I shared with God my fears. A peace that was comforting came over me. I believe he calmed my fears. When I was baptized years later, I was asked if I would accept God into my life. I told the minister I already had. It was on the deserts of Arizona.

We left for Arizona on July 9, 2005. We spent time in Sedona, Arizona. How beautiful it was. I might add that we kept a journal on our trip. We headed to Tucson and spent a very sweltering afternoon in Old Tucson Studios, and from there, we headed to Sonoita. As we were leaving Tucson, we could see a fire in the distance. We found ourselves heading in the direction of the fire. Sonoita is forty miles south of Tucson. Well, we girls joked that that couldn't be where we were heading. What would the odds of that be?

The closer we got to Sonoita, the more concerned we were with this. We pulled off the main highway onto a dirt road that led to where we once lived. We were heading west now. A few miles down the road, we came to the fork of the road that would take us to our destination. There was none other than a Road Closed sign in the middle of the road. There was no way that was happening. The fire was off to our left, and we could easily see the tanker planes but not feel that the fire was a threat to us (it was off in a good distance).

We crossed the Road Closed sign. Now we knew that if we'd get caught, we would probably get a pretty stiff fine. We were willing to risk it. That was how much it meant to us. Well, we went the couple of miles or so on this washboard road and came to the Box Canyon road sign. Right at the bend of the road was where we once lived. We made that right turn, and before us was this long (fifty-foot) strip of crime scene tape across the property. We were right there, so close we could reach out and touch it, but we weren't about to cross that tape. We weren't going to leave our DNA there. We shared how we felt that it was about time someone recognized a crime had been committed there, even if it was forty years ago. We felt so defeated. We headed back to the first fork where the Road Closed sign was and just sat there. This was happening!

A few minutes later, a BLM truck came by and headed down that washboard road. I was in the front passenger seat, so I jumped out and ran after the truck. The gentleman stopped. I told him of our plight, and he said to head to the property and he would get a permission slip made out for us. We waited at the property for a little while, and as we did, we saw another BLM truck heading in the direction of the first truck. He was heading down to sign the approval for us. We got our paper and spent a memorable hour together.

We found the tree that once held our tree house. It had grown tall, but it still had the remnants of the steps that led to the top of the tree house. We found the ditch where a colt donkey was born. The donkeys were our pets. We called them the Bell family—Jingle Bell, Lulu Bell, Mary Bell, and Tinker Bell. Just this past Christmas, my nephew Jesse bought me a donkey planter for our yard. He had just learned of my love of the donkeys and why. I named that donkey Taco Bell.

We saw the caves where we believed Dave mined out of. We saw everything but the cross. Maybe there was a fire at another time that had burned it down. Of course, there was no shack. We didn't see one scorpion, snake, or tarantula. Trust me, we looked out for them.

We headed to Tombstone with new memories of Box Canyon Road. Thank you, BLM.

PS: The crime scene tape was to keep traffic coming through from Tucson to observe the fire.

AN EARLY LIGHT

After a day at Tombstone, we headed to Telluride, Colorado, another place we had lived in with our mom and Dave. Telluride had coal mines, and Dave did mining there too. Those mountains in Telluride were as beautiful as we remembered them to be. You want to talk about winter? Go spend one in Telluride. We did in 1964–1965.

Now I have a story here that really has no bearing on any of this other than to show you I am finding the humor in things once again. That journal I have told you about would end each day with "Hot, hot, hot." After days of being in the heat of Arizona, we kept commenting on how we couldn't wait to get to Colorado. Now we were all pretty much in our early fifties and suffering hot flashes and whatnot. We needed to get to Colorado! We got to our motel at the midnight hour. The only motel rooms they had left were a couple of suites. We took one and all shared a room. In order to save time, Peggy and Barbara showered the night before. Adrienne and I showered in the morning. I got up first and showered. Well, the bathroom was like a sauna, so I turned on the little timer on the wall in the bathroom. I needed to cool it down in here. As it turned out, it wasn't air-conditioning. It was a heater. I was sweating and thinking of my poor sisters as they slept. I couldn't turn the timer off. I got the giggles so bad I had to go into the living room with my pillow to smother my laughter so as not to wake the girls. We got to Telluride the next morning, and they were having a heat wave themselves. High nineties, the shops we visited, and our motel room had no air-conditioning. Colorado was hot, hot, hot.

We've all heard the phrase "Pennies from heaven." Angel has quite a collection of them, and they are all Kelly's birth year, 1978.

There would be circumstances that would cause Angel to turn to her sister for comfort. A little later, she would discover a penny where she had just sat in, in a conversation.

Brianna and Ireland, one night, wanted to curl up in bed with Mommy to watch a movie on television. Their mommy said, "No, this movie has some scary parts in it, and it can give you nightmares."

They both said that they would ask Aunt Kelly to not let them have nightmares. Angel told the girls that Auntie Kelly was a busy girl, probably doing important stuff, and she couldn't always be here. The next morning, Angel was making up her bed, and under the covers was a 1978 penny.

Angel has many more penny stories to remind her of Kelly.

So as to not change the subject, here is an experience Randy and I just had. We had to make a trip to Reno, and while there, we ran into Lowe's to make a purchase. We had just entered the store and were in conversation with each other by the garden seed area when I saw a dime fall from above Randy's head and land at his feet. I told him what I had witnessed, and he said, "I didn't see it." About that time, a nickel bounced off my head, and he said, "I saw that!" The day before, Randy spent hours wrapping nickels and dimes we had been saving for Brianna and Ireland. They collected the quarters the last time they came to visit.

Chapter Eighteen

God's Timing

For the last couple of months, I had pretty much set this aside, intending to get back to it in due time. I wasn't being real aggressive about finishing this up. I needed to make the necessary corrections and put in order of events as they took place. That's when the work really began. It was not easy to backpedal! I really thought I had made the last entry in my book. Kelly spoke to me, "That's a pretty amazing ending." I had already felt by this time that I was only the writer of this. She was the author. She gave me the stories. She even had one more. This one, however, actually took place almost ten years ago, unbeknownst to us until just recently. This has raised a lot of questions, but my final analysis is that God's timing is always on time.

I was looking for an important document and was unable to find it in the filing cabinet. Randy had a shoe box in the bottom of his gun safe that had some important papers in it, so I pulled it out and looked through it. I noticed it had some of Kelly's bank statements, an important letter from the University of Nevada, Reno, and a couple of her high school ID cards.

There was also a five-by-seven manila envelope in that box. It was licked closed, clamped, and taped shut. I assumed it belonged to Randy. I had picked this envelope up a number of times over the last few years. Sure, I was curious, but it was in Randy's safe, so it was not my business. I knew better than to open a sealed document. There was no writing on the outside, so I left it alone. I looked through that box twice and could not find the document I was looking for. When Randy woke up, I asked him to help me look for it. He wound up looking in that same shoebox, and I told him I had already looked through it twice. He chose to look through it one more time. I left him sitting on the floor in front of his safe and headed for the kitchen. He got up, went over, and sat on the sofa. I came out of the kitchen and looked at Randy. He had an ashen look on his face.

I said, "What?"

He said, "You have to read this."

I said, "What is it?"

He said, "It's a letter from Kelly." I was shaking as I read this:

> *I can only pray that this note is not read in the near future. If it is, it means I was needed elsewhere. Remember, you are not burying or cremating my soul, only a body. Ash to ash, dust to dust. It's the circle of life. Pray for me, but do not worry. I am with my Creator, and I am happy. Remember, no tears in heaven.*
>
> *To my family, you could only know how much love I had inside for you. Thank you for everything! I will see you again. Do not forget me, but live without me.*
>
> *To my closest friends, thank you. I love and I will miss you.*
>
> *Kelly D. Tassi*
> *September 12, 1996*

WILL

Will of Kelly Dawn Tassi (11/18/78)

> *I hereby will all my belongings to Janice L. Tassi, Randy R. Tassi, Ted W. Tassi, and Angela N. Tassi.*
>
> *I also will all my love and memories to those who mean the very most to me. Those who really know me will know who they are.*
>
> *Kelly Dawn Tassi*
> *September 12, 1996*

I couldn't breathe. My face was numb. I had unbelievable chills and that haunting cry. Oh my god. Why? What? When? Where? How? So many questions. I was in shock. By this time, Randy said that nothing shocked him anymore.

It would be a half hour later that I would call Angel to share this with her. Brian answered the phone, and I was glad for that, because I knew Angel would react like me, and I wanted to reassure Brian that everything was okay here. Even though I knew I wasn't very audible, I read the letter to Brian first. He put Angel on the phone, and I was right. How do you comprehend something like that? We expected to find a letter like this and a will from our elders, not from your child. Kelly was seventeen at the time. She had graduated in 1996 and was taking a semester off before starting the junior college here. This was September of 1996. What was going on in her life at that time? Did she sense or know something? She had just gotten through Antelope, hunting the month before with her dad, and it was a successful, fun hunt. I got out her journal, and there was nothing entered in it even close to that date. I called Shannon to ask her if Kelly had shared anything with her around that time. I thought maybe Kelly would confide in her where maybe she wouldn't with us. No, Kelly hadn't shared anything with her.

Where had Kelly kept that envelope all those years before? Randy didn't get the safe until 2000. He said that Kelly had asked if she could keep that shoe box in his safe. I pulled out that box and looked through it real carefully. Kelly was class historian, so she would get monthly statements from the bank showing the monies and interest for the class of 1996. She would have been planning their tenth-year reunion this year. Shannon had taken over those duties as she was the other class historian.

I had kept those bank statements for years in a drawer in my china hutch. At one time, after her dad got this safe, she gathered up her valuable papers and put them together in that box. She intended for us to find that manila envelope someday. I often think of how many times I had that in my hand these last few years. I didn't know what I was holding. I had used every adjective there was in trying to describe this find. I might add that I had heard every adjective there was as well from others. Unbelievable.

The next day, I called my good friend Mitzie to share this with her. Her reaction was the same as everyone else's. She then said, "When did you find that letter?

I said, "Yesterday."

She said, "Do you know what yesterday was?"

I said, "Yes, it was Wednesday."

She said, "Do you know what yesterday was?"

I said, "March 1."

She said, "Jan, it was Ash Wednesday."

I said, "Oh my god, you're right."

But I didn't really have a full understanding of what Ash Wednesday was all about. She was raised Catholic, so she knew the significance of this day and this time of year. She explained it to me, and it took on a life of its own. What are the odds of finding it on that exact day? We'll never know what had provoked Kelly to write that letter and will. We only know that she had intended for us to find it someday. When she went away to school and later moved into her home with Darin, she took all her stuff, except for a few childhood possessions (stuffed animals, dolls, etc.) and some clothes in the closet. She took it all with her, except for the contents in that shoe box. Did she maybe hear a voice too? I did in 1986. This was written in 1996 and found in 2006. Maybe she just knew. Someday we will too!

Just before this discovery, Ted had shared with us that he and his wife were expecting a baby (August 14). Our grandson was born by C-section on Sunday, August 13, 2006. He weighed eleven pounds, five ounces. The exact date and hour of our loss of Kelly, our grandson was born. No, Mommy was not induced! I might add that she had been having contractions daily for over a week prior to his birth. I was staying with her at the time.

On the white roses we had for Kelly's memorial was a ribbon across them with a description we had chosen for her. It read An Angel among Us.

I was noticing the special little gestures our neighbors were doing to include us and make us feel like we belonged. There is a three-and-a-half-year-old granddaughter to our neighbors across the street. Her name is Annie, and she is just about the sweetest little girl you will ever meet. I love it when she hollers at me across the street and says, "Hi, Grandma Tassi." I have had the pleasure of seeing this little girl grow up. She was Annie Oakley last Halloween. She looks forward to Brianna and Ireland's coming next month, and they are going to have a sleepover. Her little sister, Elizabeth, is just one and half years, but I bet she will do a sleepover too someday.

So many things cause me to pause for a moment. How I will always miss what could have been. But when brought back to reality, I thank the little Annies.

"Excuse me, am I where I am supposed to be?"

Epilogue

There were so many things to be considered before publishing this. I first and foremost wanted the approval of those involved, especially Ted and Angel. I have shared this with a number of family and friends to get feedback. They all were so supportive and, where needed, were graceful in their constructive criticisms.

After learning what it would take to get a book published, I became very discouraged. So I procrastinated some more. I have been sitting on this so long. We now have a new president (Obama). Randy really wanted me to get this published, if only for us, family, friends, and some extra copies for anyone else interested in our story.

We decided to look into a self-published book, and that appeared to be the way to go. Maybe we needed this time to come full circle in the healing process. I'm anxious to share with you that Ted, Angel, and their families are all doing well. We have another grandson. Aidan Donavan Russell was born in January 2008. I believe this completes Angel and Brian's family. They are happy and busy in their lives. Angel has got some of that strength and confidence that was lost in time back. She has become more assertive and has developed that same fire and fight I have developed in me all those years ago on a walk home from school, eating my cup of ice cream. Strength is in numbers. One day at a time.

Ted and his wife are equally busy in their lives. She is a stay-at-home mom and is a loving, nurturing, and very involved mommy. I hear the love and joy in Ted's voice when he talks and shares about his family. Ted is still addressing issues that have come from his own loss, of a sister. We are so proud of him and how when he sees the need for help in one area or another, he seeks it out. He faces these challenges with great determination to overcome them. The effects of our loss of Kelly are more recognizable in Ted. He is too quiet and more reserved. He deals in his own way and time.

Shannon and Eric have two beautiful children. Reece is four years old, and his sister, Brynn, is a year and a half. We are happy to be Grandma and Grandpa to them, along with being biological grandparents. Our time together is very special. Denielle and Remo have a sweet little girl, Cicily, born on July 4, 2006. We keep in touch and see each other on occasion, but not as often as we like. Sister Sue is a wonderful part of our lives. Enid (from the rest home) has passed away a few springs ago. She has joined her three sons and husband, who have gone before her. Their chain has been linked back together again.

Darin and Michelle are expecting their first child in October. I love how the communication lines remain open with Darin. He still calls us Mom and Dad. Dorothy is eighty-five years old and still very entertaining.

Clyde McPotts had been up for parole a few weeks ago. Randy, Darin, and I went to the parole board hearing. We sat before the members of the board and expressed our anger and concerns about an early release for someone who had shown no remorse for what he had done to Kelly and how we felt he would be a threat to the public. Ten days later, we got the letter informing us that Clyde was denied parole and would not be eligible again for three more years. There was a good possibility he could get out then, but not today. The maximum he could serve, or we can keep him in prison for, would be the year 2014.

Today I am involved with an organization called NOPE (Narcotics Overdose Prevention and Education). We are a small group of people with a big job: educating children at the junior and high school level about the effects of drugs. We have speakers (mothers) sharing their stories on their loss of a child from drug overdose.

There are tragic stories, shared across the map, of loved ones lost due to addiction or accidental overdose.

We do the whole nine yards and hold very little back on getting the point across to these kids. I have spoken a few times myself about the tragic loss of our daughter. So, so difficult.

I was recently asked to speak for Every 15 Minutes, put on by the California Highway Patrol. They do reenactments of auto accidents caused by drunk/drug-influenced drivers—very impactful and emotional. Like in NOPE, a lot of kids walk away crying. Sometimes the most difficult things we do in life are the most important ones.

Randy and I went to see a medium a few years ago, and what an awesome experience. Randy, being the skeptic, thought for sure the guy was going to trip up. He was so impressed. I've always believed that there are those with special gifts, so I have always been open to the possibility. We had a one-hour one-on-one with the gentleman and walked away with God bumps. We had the session taped and went on to have it transcribed. The medium was a good 90 percent accurate on events, names, dates, and eerily, the description of the accident. If we'd have the opportunity to do that again, we'd do it in a heartbeat!

The year is 2009, and as a country and a nation, we are all faced with some of the most difficult challenges and losses we have seen in decades, if not ever.

With a bad stimulus plan, unemployment at a record high, home foreclosures, bankruptcies, etc., how can we not be disappointed in a government and state systems we have put so much trust in? We need some more of that time!

There is still some good news out there though. We just have to dig a little deeper to find it or reach a little higher and embrace it.

Epilogue II

As you can see, *An Early Light* has a long shelf life. It has been back on that shelf for six more years. Learning that I was going to have to take out or change our grandkids' names really threw me. It hurt that our daughter-in-law wished our grandson was not born on *that day*. We all saw the gift in it as it gave us a reason to celebrate instead of mourn that day. Our grandkids are not a part of the tragedy of this but a part of the healing of it. I wish she could see that, but we all do what we have to do to protect our own, and I get that. So I put this aside, hoping she would change her mind, then stubbornly refused to make the changes and omissions when I didn't hear back from her. We have never spoken of this matter since.

Ted and his wife just recently divorced. We love our daughter-in-law and hope to have a continued relationship with her. We are all going to Lagoon, a Six Flags park in Salt Lake City, Utah, in a couple of weeks. We have done this a few times as the grandkids have a blast there, and we are all together. That is always a good day. Angel, Brian, and family are all doing well. They are part of this trip to Lagoon also, so we will see them soon.

Randy and I are doing good and are always busy. He retired a few years ago and never sits still. I can't keep up with him. Our days are full, and when we are free from our responsibilities, we love hanging out with our dear best friends, Rocky and Debbie. We have shared many tears of sorrow and difficulties and have loved and supported each other in emergency situations, pulling all-nighters in a hospital waiting room. We have shared tears of joy and laughter. We have laughed longer and harder with these two friends, and the joke is usually directed at ourselves. We are actually very entertaining, even if we are the only ones to see it or admit it. We are able to laugh at ourselves because we know how to find humor in so many situations.

Rode elevators up and down, up and down in search of the two who exited because they were sure they had the right floor, and they did, while the other two stubbornly hated to admit it. We found ourselves straddled on railroad tracks when we thought another driver was not going to share pavement in Pennsylvania. We'd been stranded together in an airport in Germany due to ash from a nearby volcanic eruption. We mixed-matched shoes while dressing in semidarkness, only to be discovered hours later in the daylight, miles and hours from home. I will not name names, but I always check my shoes before I leave home now. Randy double-checks my shoes too. Doesn't hurt to get a second opinion.

We have families of wildlife out our back door, so they are a good distraction from me getting a lot accomplished indoors. Herds of deer with new fawns in the spring. Hundreds of geese, ducks, quail, and doves, to name but a few feathered friends. An occasional eagle swooping down on the pond for its next meal. Jackrabbits, squirrels, raccoons, fox, and yes, skunks. We have seen evidence of mountain lions but have had no confrontations. Those squirrels I have mentioned have become overpopulated, so last summer, Randy started setting traps to thin them out here and deposit them at a nearby mountainous area. He once trapped a fox and freed him to roam again, as well as a skunk.

How do you set a skunk free? Very carefully! First, you warn your neighbors and then wait for morning golfers to clear the course. You then tie a hundred feet or so of rope to a cage, attach it to the hitch on the back of a Polaris (a four-wheeler will do), very carefully unlatch the cage door, get back in Polaris, gun it, and do not stop until you see a skunk flying through the air and landing on his feet, running for his life. No time to even think of raising his tail! This was a low-ceiling cage, so he was unable to raise his tail while in it. No animals were hurt while doing this, but we sure made a few neighbors nervous. We had company at the time with kids, who got a kick out of this. We were all just ready to run.

There is never a dull moment around here, and we have the most amazing sunsets on a very busy pond. Kind of cool to watch helicopters dip into it to dash a nearby summer fire. It has seen rafts, canoes, sailboats, Jet Skis, ski boats, and swimmers over the years, plus a few brave ice-skaters in the winter. We are greatly and richly entertained, and we don't ever take that for granted.

Darin and Michelle have two of the sweetest little boys, Ethan (five years) and Nathan (three years). We are Grandma and Grandpa to them, and they just came and spent ten days with us while Mommy and Daddy went on vacation. We love these boys as well as Darin and Michelle. Michelle is like a daughter-in-law to us. We have grown together through this. Darin now works for Sparks Fire Department and has just made fire chief there. Michelle works for University of Nevada, Reno.

Shannon and her husband, Eric, are very busy with jobs and three children, Reece (ten years), Brynn (seven years), and Van (four years), whom we are very proud to call our grandkids. Shannon is back to work on this for me. I couldn't have done any of this without her. Oh so grateful. All this because we did not close the doors to the possibilities.

In the last few years, I have lost a sister, a father, and a stepmother. In January, we had to put my mom in a nursing home. In February, we put Dorothy (the dragon lady) in our local nursing and rehabilitation home. So goes life. How far have we all traveled from 2009 to today, 2015, since all that "hope and change" was promised to us? Far and away! Where will we find the hope when we are removing it from the schools, having to take it down from a Christmas scene or out of a Christmas program and holiday greeting? I would rather hear "Merry [Mary] had a little lamb" (that she did) instead of "Happy Holidays." We didn't need change. We just needed improvements. We were already good. Look where all that change has gotten us. We see the effects of it every day on any news station or any newspaper.

We need a president who will lead us, not deliver us. When those planes brought down the Twin Towers, they brought America to her knees. I was raised a Democrat but changed my ticket because I wanted to stand behind a president who would stand up for America. That pendulum swings both ways. We just got to get it together, together. We used to solve so much around the dinner table, talk things through in a meeting room with a meeting of minds, resolve issues with a manner of respect, or address a fight with a fist, not a gun. While we fear someone making or detonating that big bomb, we do not realize that there is a little one housed inside us, waiting for someone or something to ignite it. Whether it be race, religion, or politics, we need to diffuse that bomb inside us because that is a fire we cannot put out. If we continue to rise up against one another, we will be brought to our knees once again.

CPSIA information can be obtained
at www.ICGtesting.com
Printed in the USA
FSOW01n0710280815
10406FS

9 781503 592797